Index

Important Notice

These tables cover the main rates of tax included in the Finance Act 2018 and those announced by the Chancellor of the Exchequer in the Autumn Budget on 29 October 2018.

The rates apply for 2018/19 and 2019/20 (subject to enactment), and for the corporation tax financial years 2018 and 2019.

How to use these tables for pence

These tables can be used for calculation in £, in pence, or in a combination of £ and pence.

Examples:

Page 8 20% of £28 = £5·60
20% of 28p = 5·6p = 6p to nearest penny.

Page 18 What is the VAT content at 20% of an inclusive price of £50·83p?

£50·00	=		£8·33
0·83	=	13·83p =	0·14
£50·83	=		£8.47

AF778182

General Editor
Mark McLaughlin CTA (Fellow) ATT (Fellow) TEP, Mark McLaughlin Associates Ltd

Original Contributors
Personal tax
Sarah Laing CTA, Technical Author
National Insurance
Sarah Bradford BA Hons ACA CTA (Fellow)
Stamp taxes
Shimon Shaw, VWV
Pensions
Sarah Bradford BA Hons ACA CTA (Fellow)
Corporate tax
Satwaki Chanda, Barrister at Law
Capital taxes
Rebecca Cave FCA CTA MBA and Sarah Bradford BA Hons ACA CTA (Fellow)
VAT
Andrew Needham BA CTA, VAT Specialists Ltd
Customs duties
Andrew Needham BA CTA, VAT Specialists Ltd
Anti-avoidance and HMRC administration
Satwaki Chanda, Barrister at Law and Sarah Bradford BA Hons ACA CTA (Fellow)

Bloomsbury Professional

Maxwelton House, 41–43 Boltro Road,
Haywards Heath, West Sussex, RH16 1BJ

Bloomsbury Professional, an imprint of Bloomsbury Publishing Plc

ISBN 978 1 52650 934 5

Typeset by Evolution Design & Digital Ltd (Kent)
Printed in the United Kingdom by Bell & Bain Ltd.

Gifts to Charities – net cost for individuals from 6 April 2018

By donations via Gift Aid and by deduction from pay under the Payroll Giving Schemes.

Gross amount received by Charity	Net cost to Donor Top rate of income tax		Gross amount received by Charity	Net cost to Donor Top rate of income tax	
	20%	40%		20%	40%
£	£	£	**£**	£	£
1	0·80	0·60	**51**	40·80	30·60
2	1·60	1·20	**52**	41·60	31·20
3	2·40	1·80	**53**	42·40	31·80
4	3·20	2·40	**54**	43·20	32·40
5	4·00	3·00	**55**	44·00	33·00
6	4·80	3·60	**56**	44·80	33·60
7	5·60	4·20	**57**	45·60	34·20
8	6·40	4·80	**58**	46·40	34·80
9	7·20	5·40	**59**	47·20	35·40
10	8·00	6·00	**60**	48·00	36·00
11	8·80	6·60	**61**	48·80	36·60
12	9·60	7·20	**62**	49·60	37·20
13	10·40	7·80	**63**	50·40	37·80
14	11·20	8·40	**64**	51·20	38·40
15	12·00	9·00	**65**	52·00	39·00
16	12·80	9·60	**66**	52·80	39·60
17	13·60	10·20	**67**	53·60	40·20
18	14·40	10·80	**68**	54·40	40·80
19	15·20	11·40	**69**	55·20	41·40
20	16·00	12·00	**70**	56·00	42·00
21	16·80	12·60	**71**	56·80	42·60
22	17·60	13·20	**72**	57·60	43·20
23	18·40	13·80	**73**	58·40	43·80
24	19·20	14·40	**74**	59·20	44·40
25	20·00	15·00	**75**	60·00	45·00
26	20·80	15·60	**76**	60·80	45·60
27	21·60	16·20	**77**	61·60	46·20
28	22·40	16·80	**78**	62·40	46·80
29	23·20	17·40	**79**	63·20	47·40
30	24·00	18·00	**80**	64·00	48·00
31	24·80	18·60	**81**	64·80	48·60
32	25·60	19·20	**82**	65·60	49·20
33	26·40	19·80	**83**	66·40	49·80
34	27·20	20·40	**84**	67·20	50·40
35	28·00	21·00	**85**	68·00	51·00
36	28·80	21·60	**86**	68·80	51·60
37	29·60	22·20	**87**	69·60	52·20
38	30·40	22·80	**88**	70·40	52·80
39	31·20	23·40	**89**	71·20	53·40
40	32·00	24·00	**90**	72·00	54·00
41	32·80	24·60	**91**	72·80	54·60
42	33·60	25·20	**92**	73·60	55·20
43	34·40	25·80	**93**	74·40	55·80
44	35·20	26·40	**94**	75·20	56·40
45	36·00	27·00	**95**	76·00	57·00
46	36·80	27·60	**96**	76·80	57·60
47	37·60	28·20	**97**	77·60	58·20
48	38·40	28·80	**98**	78·40	58·80
49	39·20	29·40	**99**	79·20	59·40
50	40·00	30·00	**100**	80·00	60·00

Net cost to Donor	Gross amount received by Charity, if Donor's top rate of income tax		Net cost to Donor	Gross amount received by Charity, if Donor's top rate of income tax	
	20%	40%		20%	40%
£	£	£	**£**	£	£
1	1·25	1·67	**51**	63·75	85·00
2	2·50	3·33	**52**	65·00	86·67
3	3·75	5·00	**53**	66·25	88·33
4	5·00	6·67	**54**	67·50	90·00
5	6·25	8·33	**55**	68·75	91·67
6	7·50	10·00	**56**	70·00	93·33
7	8·75	11·67	**57**	71·25	95·00
8	10·00	13·33	**58**	72·50	96·67
9	11·25	15·00	**59**	73·75	98·33
10	12·50	16·67	**60**	75·00	100·00
11	13·75	18·33	**61**	76·25	101·67
12	15·00	20·00	**62**	77·50	103·33
13	16·25	21·67	**63**	78·75	105·00
14	17·50	23·33	**64**	80·00	106·67
15	18·75	25·00	**65**	81·25	108·33
16	20·00	26·67	**66**	82·50	110·00
17	21·25	28·33	**67**	83·75	111·67
18	22·50	30·00	**68**	85·00	113·33
19	23·75	31·67	**69**	86·25	115·00
20	25·00	33·33	**70**	87·50	116·67
21	26·25	35·00	**71**	88·75	118·33
22	27·50	36·67	**72**	90·00	120·00
23	28·75	38·33	**73**	91·25	121·67
24	30·00	40·00	**74**	92·50	123·33
25	31·25	41·67	**75**	93·75	125·00
26	32·50	43·33	**76**	95·00	126·67
27	33·75	45·00	**77**	96·25	128·33
28	35·00	46·67	**78**	97·50	130·00
29	36·25	48·33	**79**	98·75	131·67
30	37·50	50·00	**80**	100·00	133·33
31	38·75	51·67	**81**	101·25	135·00
32	40·00	53·33	**82**	102·50	136·67
33	41·25	55·00	**83**	103·75	138·33
34	42·50	56·67	**84**	105·00	140·00
35	43·75	58·33	**85**	106·25	141·67
36	45·00	60·00	**86**	107·50	143·33
37	46·25	61·67	**87**	108·75	145·00
38	47·50	63·33	**88**	110·00	146·67
39	48·75	65·00	**89**	111·25	148·33
40	50·00	66·67	**90**	112·50	150·00
41	51·25	68·33	**91**	113·75	151·67
42	52·50	70·00	**92**	115·00	153·33
43	53·75	71·67	**93**	116·25	155·00
44	55·00	73·33	**94**	117·50	156·67
45	56·25	75·00	**95**	118·75	158·33
46	57·50	76·67	**96**	120·00	160·00
47	58·75	78·33	**97**	121·25	161·67
48	60·00	80·00	**98**	122·50	163·33
49	61·25	81·67	**99**	123·75	165·00
50	62·50	83·33	**100**	125·00	166·67

7.5%   2018/19 and 2019/20: Income Tax on Dividend Income

Payable by basic rate taxpayers on dividends exceeding the dividend allowance. (Note: The dividend allowance has been reduced from £5,000 to £2,000 for 2018/19 onwards).

£ or p	Tax £ or p	£ or p	Tax £ or p	£	Tax £	£	Tax £	£	Tax £	£	Tax £	£	Tax £	£	Tax £	£	Tax £	£	Tax £
1	0·08	**51**	3·83	**101**	7·58	**151**	11·33	**201**	15·08	**251**	18·83	**301**	22·58	**351**	26·33	**401**	30·08	**451**	33·83
2	0·15	**52**	3·90	**102**	7·65	**152**	11·40	**202**	15·15	**252**	18·90	**302**	22·65	**352**	26·40	**402**	30·15	**452**	33·90
3	0·23	**53**	3·98	**103**	7·73	**153**	11·48	**203**	15·23	**253**	18·98	**303**	22·73	**353**	26·48	**403**	30·23	**453**	33·98
4	0·30	**54**	4·05	**104**	7·80	**154**	11·55	**204**	15·30	**254**	19·05	**304**	22·80	**354**	26·55	**404**	30·30	**454**	34·05
5	0·38	**55**	4·13	**105**	7·88	**155**	11·63	**205**	15·38	**255**	19·13	**305**	22·88	**355**	26·63	**405**	30·38	**455**	34·13
6	0·45	**56**	4·20	**106**	7·95	**156**	11·70	**206**	15·45	**256**	19·20	**306**	22·95	**356**	26·70	**406**	30·45	**456**	34·20
7	0·53	**57**	4·28	**107**	8·03	**157**	11·78	**207**	15·53	**257**	19·28	**307**	23·03	**357**	26·78	**407**	30·53	**457**	34·28
8	0·60	**58**	4·35	**108**	8·10	**158**	11·85	**208**	15·60	**258**	19·35	**308**	23·10	**358**	26·85	**408**	30·60	**458**	34·35
9	0·68	**59**	4·43	**109**	8·18	**159**	11·93	**209**	15·68	**259**	19·43	**309**	23·18	**359**	26·93	**409**	30·68	**459**	34·43
10	0·75	**60**	4·50	**110**	8·25	**160**	12·00	**210**	15·75	**260**	19·50	**310**	23·25	**360**	27·00	**410**	30·75	**460**	34·50
11	0·83	**61**	4·58	**111**	8·33	**161**	12·08	**211**	15·83	**261**	19·58	**311**	23·33	**361**	27·08	**411**	30·83	**461**	34·58
12	0·90	**62**	4·65	**112**	8·40	**162**	12·15	**212**	15·90	**262**	19·65	**312**	23·40	**362**	27·15	**412**	30·90	**462**	34·65
13	0·98	**63**	4·73	**113**	8·48	**163**	12·23	**213**	15·98	**263**	19·73	**313**	23·48	**363**	27·23	**413**	30·98	**463**	34·73
14	1·05	**64**	4·80	**114**	8·55	**164**	12·30	**214**	16·05	**264**	19·80	**314**	23·55	**364**	27·30	**414**	31·05	**464**	34·80
15	1·13	**65**	4·88	**115**	8·63	**165**	12·38	**215**	16·13	**265**	19·88	**315**	23·63	**365**	27·38	**415**	31·13	**465**	34·88
16	1·20	**66**	4·95	**116**	8·70	**166**	12·45	**216**	16·20	**266**	19·95	**316**	23·70	**366**	27·45	**416**	31·20	**466**	34·95
17	1·28	**67**	5·03	**117**	8·78	**167**	12·53	**217**	16·28	**267**	20·03	**317**	23·78	**367**	27·53	**417**	31·28	**467**	35·03
18	1·35	**68**	5·10	**118**	8·85	**168**	12·60	**218**	16·35	**268**	20·10	**318**	23·85	**368**	27·60	**418**	31·35	**468**	35·10
19	1·43	**69**	5·18	**119**	8·93	**169**	12·68	**219**	16·43	**269**	20·18	**319**	23·93	**369**	27·68	**419**	31·43	**469**	35·18
20	1·50	**70**	5·25	**120**	9·00	**170**	12·75	**220**	16·50	**270**	20·25	**320**	24·00	**370**	27·75	**420**	31·50	**470**	35·25
21	1·58	**71**	5·33	**121**	9·08	**171**	12·83	**221**	16·58	**271**	20·33	**321**	24·08	**371**	27·83	**421**	31·58	**471**	35·33
22	1·65	**72**	5·40	**122**	9·15	**172**	12·90	**222**	16·65	**272**	20·40	**322**	24·15	**372**	27·90	**422**	31·65	**472**	35·40
23	1·73	**73**	5·48	**123**	9·23	**173**	12·98	**223**	16·73	**273**	20·48	**323**	24·23	**373**	27·98	**423**	31·73	**473**	35·48
24	1·80	**74**	5·55	**124**	9·30	**174**	13·05	**224**	16·80	**274**	20·55	**324**	24·30	**374**	28·05	**424**	31·80	**474**	35·55
25	1·88	**75**	5·63	**125**	9·38	**175**	13·13	**225**	16·88	**275**	20·63	**325**	24·38	**375**	28·13	**425**	31·88	**475**	35·63
26	1·95	**76**	5·70	**126**	9·45	**176**	13·20	**226**	16·95	**276**	20·70	**326**	24·45	**376**	28·20	**426**	31·95	**476**	35·70
27	2·03	**77**	5·78	**127**	9·53	**177**	13·28	**227**	17·03	**277**	20·78	**327**	24·53	**377**	28·28	**427**	32·03	**477**	35·78
28	2·10	**78**	5·85	**128**	9·60	**178**	13·35	**228**	17·10	**278**	20·85	**328**	24·60	**378**	28·35	**428**	32·10	**478**	35·85
29	2·18	**79**	5·93	**129**	9·68	**179**	13·43	**229**	17·18	**279**	20·93	**329**	24·68	**379**	28·43	**429**	32·18	**479**	35·93
30	2·25	**80**	6·00	**130**	9·75	**180**	13·50	**230**	17·25	**280**	21·00	**330**	24·75	**380**	28·50	**430**	32·25	**480**	36·00
31	2·33	**81**	6·08	**131**	9·83	**181**	13·58	**231**	17·33	**281**	21·08	**331**	24·83	**381**	28·58	**431**	32·33	**481**	36·08
32	2·40	**82**	6·15	**132**	9·90	**182**	13·65	**232**	17·40	**282**	21·15	**332**	24·90	**382**	28·65	**432**	32·40	**482**	36·15
33	2·48	**83**	6·23	**133**	9·98	**183**	13·73	**233**	17·48	**283**	21·23	**333**	24·98	**383**	28·73	**433**	32·48	**483**	36·23
34	2·55	**84**	6·30	**134**	10·05	**184**	13·80	**234**	17·55	**284**	21·30	**334**	25·05	**384**	28·80	**434**	32·55	**484**	36·30
35	2·63	**85**	6·38	**135**	10·13	**185**	13·88	**235**	17·63	**285**	21·38	**335**	25·13	**385**	28·88	**435**	32·63	**485**	36·38
36	2·70	**86**	6·45	**136**	10·20	**186**	13·95	**236**	17·70	**286**	21·45	**336**	25·20	**386**	28·95	**436**	32·70	**486**	36·45
37	2·78	**87**	6·53	**137**	10·28	**187**	14·03	**237**	17·78	**287**	21·53	**337**	25·28	**387**	29·03	**437**	32·78	**487**	36·53
38	2·85	**88**	6·60	**138**	10·35	**188**	14·10	**238**	17·85	**288**	21·60	**338**	25·35	**388**	29·10	**438**	32·85	**488**	36·60
39	2·93	**89**	6·68	**139**	10·43	**189**	14·18	**239**	17·93	**289**	21·68	**339**	25·43	**389**	29·18	**439**	32·93	**489**	36·68
40	3·00	**90**	6·75	**140**	10·50	**190**	14·25	**240**	18·00	**290**	21·75	**340**	25·50	**390**	29·25	**440**	33·00	**490**	36·75
41	3·08	**91**	6·83	**141**	10·58	**191**	14·33	**241**	18·08	**291**	21·83	**341**	25·58	**391**	29·33	**441**	33·08	**491**	36·83
42	3·15	**92**	6·90	**142**	10·65	**192**	14·40	**242**	18·15	**292**	21·90	**342**	25·65	**392**	29·40	**442**	33·15	**492**	36·90
43	3·23	**93**	6·98	**143**	10·73	**193**	14·48	**243**	18·23	**293**	21·98	**343**	25·73	**393**	29·48	**443**	33·23	**493**	36·98
44	3·30	**94**	7·05	**144**	10·80	**194**	14·55	**244**	18·30	**294**	22·05	**344**	25·80	**394**	29·55	**444**	33·30	**494**	37·05
45	3·38	**95**	7·13	**145**	10·88	**195**	14·63	**245**	18·38	**295**	22·13	**345**	25·88	**395**	29·63	**445**	33·38	**495**	37·13
46	3·45	**96**	7·20	**146**	10·95	**196**	14·70	**246**	18·45	**296**	22·20	**346**	25·95	**396**	29·70	**446**	33·45	**496**	37·20
47	3·53	**97**	7·28	**147**	11·03	**197**	14·78	**247**	18·53	**297**	22·28	**347**	26·03	**397**	29·78	**447**	33·53	**497**	37·28
48	3·60	**98**	7·35	**148**	11·10	**198**	14·85	**248**	18·60	**298**	22·35	**348**	26·10	**398**	29·85	**448**	33·60	**498**	37·35
49	3·68	**99**	7·43	**149**	11·18	**199**	14·93	**249**	18·68	**299**	22·43	**349**	26·18	**399**	29·93	**449**	33·68	**499**	37·43
50	3·75	**100**	7·50	**150**	11·25	**200**	15·00	**250**	18·75	**300**	22·50	**350**	26·25	**400**	30·00	**450**	33·75	**500**	37·50
On Tax		**£1,000** £75·00		**£1,500** £112·50		**£2,000** £150·00		**£2,500** £187·50		**£3,000** £225·00		**£3,500** £262·50		**£4,000** £300·00		**£4,500** £337·50		**£5,000** £375	

Payable by basic rate taxpayers on dividends exceeding the dividend allowance. (Note: The dividend allowance has been reduced from £5,000 to £2,000 for 2018/19 onwards).

2018/19 and 2019/20: Income Tax on Dividend Income 7.5%

£ or p	Tax £ or p	£ or p	Tax £ or p	£	Tax £	£	Tax £	£	Tax £	£	Tax £	£	Tax £	£	Tax £	£	Tax £	£	Tax £
501	37·58	551	41·33	601	45·08	651	48·83	701	52·58	751	56·33	801	60·08	851	63·83	901	67·58	951	71·33
502	37·65	552	41·40	602	45·15	652	48·90	702	52·65	752	56·40	802	60·15	852	63·90	902	67·65	952	71·40
503	37·73	553	41·48	603	45·23	653	48·98	703	52·73	753	56·48	803	60·23	853	63·98	903	67·73	953	71·48
504	37·80	554	41·55	604	45·30	654	49·05	704	52·80	754	56·55	804	60·30	854	64·05	904	67·80	954	71·55
505	37·88	555	41·63	605	45·38	655	49·13	705	52·88	755	56·63	805	60·38	855	64·13	905	67·88	955	71·63
506	37·95	556	41·70	606	45·45	656	49·20	706	52·95	756	56·70	806	60·45	856	64·20	906	67·95	956	71·70
507	38·03	557	41·78	607	45·53	657	49·28	707	53·03	757	56·78	807	60·53	857	64·28	907	68·03	957	71·78
508	38·10	558	41·85	608	45·60	658	49·35	708	53·10	758	56·85	808	60·60	858	64·35	908	68·10	958	71·85
509	38·18	559	41·93	609	45·68	659	49·43	709	53·18	759	56·93	809	60·68	859	64·43	909	68·18	959	71·93
510	38·25	560	42·00	610	45·75	660	49·50	710	53·25	760	57·00	810	60·75	860	64·50	910	68·25	960	72·00
511	38·33	561	42·08	611	45·83	661	49·58	711	53·33	761	57·08	811	60·83	861	64·58	911	68·33	961	72·08
512	38·40	562	42·15	612	45·90	662	49·65	712	53·40	762	57·15	812	60·90	862	64·65	912	68·40	962	72·15
513	38·48	563	42·23	613	45·98	663	49·73	713	53·48	763	57·23	813	60·98	863	64·73	913	68·48	963	72·23
514	38·55	564	42·30	614	46·05	664	49·80	714	53·55	764	57·30	814	61·05	864	64·80	914	68·55	964	72·30
515	38·63	565	42·38	615	46·13	665	49·88	715	53·63	765	57·38	815	61·13	865	64·88	915	68·63	965	72·38
516	38·70	566	42·45	616	46·20	666	49·95	716	53·70	766	57·45	816	61·20	866	64·95	916	68·70	966	72·45
517	38·78	567	42·53	617	46·28	667	50·03	717	53·78	767	57·53	817	61·28	867	65·03	917	68·78	967	72·53
518	38·85	568	42·60	618	46·35	668	50·10	718	53·85	768	57·60	818	61·35	868	65·10	918	68·85	968	72·60
519	38·93	569	42·68	619	46·43	669	50·18	719	53·93	769	57·68	819	61·43	869	65·18	919	68·93	969	72·68
520	39·00	570	42·75	620	46·50	670	50·25	720	54·00	770	57·75	820	61·50	870	65·25	920	69·00	970	72·75
521	39·08	571	42·83	621	46·58	671	50·33	721	54·08	771	57·83	821	61·58	871	65·33	921	69·08	971	72·83
522	39·15	572	42·90	622	46·65	672	50·40	722	54·15	772	57·90	822	61·65	872	65·40	922	69·15	972	72·90
523	39·23	573	42·98	623	46·73	673	50·48	723	54·23	773	57·98	823	61·73	873	65·48	923	69·23	973	72·98
524	39·30	574	43·05	624	46·80	674	50·55	724	54·30	774	58·05	824	61·80	874	65·55	924	69·30	974	73·05
525	39·38	575	43·13	625	46·88	675	50·63	725	54·38	775	58·13	825	61·88	875	65·63	925	69·38	975	73·13
526	39·45	576	43·20	626	46·95	676	50·70	726	54·45	776	58·20	826	61·95	876	65·70	926	69·45	976	73·20
527	39·53	577	43·28	627	47·03	677	50·78	727	54·53	777	58·28	827	62·03	877	65·78	927	69·53	977	73·28
528	39·60	578	43·35	628	47·10	678	50·85	728	54·60	778	58·35	828	62·10	878	65·85	928	69·60	978	73·35
529	39·68	579	43·43	629	47·18	679	50·93	729	54·68	779	58·43	829	62·18	879	65·93	929	69·68	979	73·43
530	39·75	580	43·50	630	47·25	680	51·00	730	54·75	780	58·50	830	62·25	880	66·00	930	69·75	980	73·50
531	39·83	581	43·58	631	47·33	681	51·08	731	54·83	781	58·58	831	62·33	881	66·08	931	69·83	981	73·58
532	39·90	582	43·65	632	47·40	682	51·15	732	54·90	782	58·65	832	62·40	882	66·15	932	69·90	982	73·65
533	39·98	583	43·73	633	47·48	683	51·23	733	54·98	783	58·73	833	62·48	883	66·23	933	69·98	983	73·73
534	40·05	584	43·80	634	47·55	684	51·30	734	55·05	784	58·80	834	62·55	884	66·30	934	70·05	984	73·80
535	40·13	585	43·88	635	47·63	685	51·38	735	55·13	785	58·88	835	62·63	885	66·38	935	70·13	985	73·88
536	40·20	586	43·95	636	47·70	686	51·45	736	55·20	786	58·95	836	62·70	886	66·45	936	70·20	986	73·95
537	40·28	587	44·03	637	47·78	687	51·53	737	55·28	787	59·03	837	62·78	887	66·53	937	70·28	987	74·03
538	40·35	588	44·10	638	47·85	688	51·60	738	55·35	788	59·10	838	62·85	888	66·60	938	70·35	988	74·10
539	40·43	589	44·18	639	47·93	689	51·68	739	55·43	789	59·18	839	62·93	889	66·68	939	70·43	989	74·18
540	40·50	590	44·25	640	48·00	690	51·75	740	55·50	790	59·25	840	63·00	890	66·75	940	70·50	990	74·25
541	40·58	591	44·33	641	48·08	69	5·18	741	55·58	791	59·33	841	63·08	891	66·83	941	70·58	991	74·33
542	40·65	592	44·40	642	48·15	692	51·90	742	55·65	792	59·40	842	63·15	892	66·90	942	70·65	992	74·40
543	40·73	593	44·48	643	48·23	693	51·98	743	55·73	793	59·48	843	63·23	893	66·98	943	70·73	993	74·48
544	40·80	594	44·55	644	48·30	694	52·05	744	55·80	794	59·55	844	63·30	894	67·05	944	70·80	994	74·55
545	40·88	595	44·63	645	48·38	695	52·13	745	55·88	795	59·63	845	63·38	895	67·13	945	70·88	995	74·63
546	40·95	596	44·70	646	48·45	696	52·20	746	55·95	796	59·70	846	63·45	896	67·20	946	70·95	996	74·70
547	41·03	597	44·78	647	48·53	697	52·28	747	56·03	797	59·78	847	63·53	897	67·28	947	71·03	997	74·78
548	41·10	598	44·85	648	48·60	698	52·35	748	56·10	798	59·85	848	63·60	898	67·35	948	71·10	998	74·85
549	41·18	599	44·93	649	48·68	699	52·43	749	56·18	799	59·93	849	63·68	899	67·43	949	71·18	999	74·93
550	41·25	600	45·00	650	48·75	700	52·50	750	56·25	800	60·00	850	63·75	900	67·50	950	71·25	1000	75·00
On		£5,500		£6,000		£6,500		£7,000		£7,500		£8,000		£8,500		£9,000		£9,500	
Tax		£412·50		£450·00		£487·50		£525·00		£562·50		£600·00		£637·50		£675·00		£712·50	

10% 2018/19 and 2019/20: Rate for capital gains qualifying for Entrepreneurs' Relief/Investors' Relief and main capital gains tax rate payable by basic rate taxpayers

£ or p	Tax £ or p	£ or p	Tax £ or p	£	Tax £	£	Tax £	£	Tax £	£	Tax £	£	Tax £	£	Tax £	£	Tax £	£	Tax £
1	0·10	51	5·10	101	10·10	151	15·10	201	20·10	251	25·10	301	30·10	351	35·10	401	40·10	451	45·10
2	0·20	52	5·20	102	10·20	152	15·20	202	20·20	252	25·20	302	30·20	352	35·20	402	40·20	452	45·20
3	0·30	53	5·30	103	10·30	153	15·30	203	20·30	253	25·30	303	30·30	353	35·30	403	40·30	453	45·30
4	0·40	54	5·40	104	10·40	154	15·40	204	20·40	254	25·40	304	30·40	354	35·40	404	40·40	454	45·40
5	0·50	55	5·50	105	10·50	155	15·50	205	20·50	255	25·50	305	30·50	355	35·50	405	40·50	455	45·50
6	0·60	56	5·60	106	10·60	156	15·60	206	20·60	256	25·60	306	30·60	356	35·60	406	40·60	456	45·60
7	0·70	57	5·70	107	10·70	157	15·70	207	20·70	257	25·70	307	30·70	357	35·70	407	40·70	457	45·70
8	0·80	58	5·80	108	10·80	158	15·80	208	20·80	258	25·80	308	30·80	358	35·80	408	40·80	458	45·80
9	0·90	59	5·90	109	10·90	159	15·90	209	20·90	259	25·90	309	30·90	359	35·90	409	40·90	459	45·90
10	1·00	60	6·00	110	11·00	160	16·00	210	21·00	260	26·00	310	31·00	360	36·00	410	41·00	460	46·00
11	1·10	61	6·10	111	11·10	161	16·10	211	21·10	261	26·10	311	31·10	361	36·10	411	41·10	461	46·10
12	1·20	62	6·20	112	11·20	162	16·20	212	21·20	262	26·20	312	31·20	362	36·20	412	41·20	462	46·20
13	1·30	63	6·30	113	11·30	163	16·30	213	21·30	263	26·30	313	31·30	363	36·30	413	41·30	463	46·30
14	1·40	64	6·40	114	11·40	164	16·40	214	21·40	264	26·40	314	31·40	364	36·40	414	41·40	464	46·40
15	1·50	65	6·50	115	11·50	165	16·50	215	21·50	265	26·50	315	31·50	365	36·50	415	41·50	465	46·50
16	1·60	66	6·60	116	11·60	166	16·60	216	21·60	266	26·60	316	31·60	366	36·60	416	41·60	466	46·60
17	1·70	67	6·70	117	11·70	167	16·70	217	21·70	267	26·70	317	31·70	367	36·70	417	41·70	467	46·70
18	1·80	68	6·80	118	11·80	168	16·80	218	21·80	268	26·80	318	31·80	368	36·80	418	41·80	468	46·80
19	1·90	69	6·90	119	11·90	169	16·90	219	21·90	269	26·90	319	31·90	369	36·90	419	41·90	469	46·90
20	2·00	70	7·00	120	12·00	170	17·00	220	22·00	270	27·00	320	32·00	370	37·00	420	42·00	470	47·00
21	2·10	71	7·10	121	12·10	171	17·10	221	22·10	271	27·10	321	32·10	371	37·10	421	42·10	471	47·10
22	2·20	72	7·20	122	12·20	172	17·20	222	22·20	272	27·20	322	32·20	372	37·20	422	42·20	472	47·20
23	2·30	73	7·30	123	12·30	173	17·30	223	22·30	273	27·30	323	32·30	373	37·30	423	42·30	473	47·30
24	2·40	74	7·40	124	12·40	174	17·40	224	22·40	274	27·40	324	32·40	374	37·40	424	42·40	474	47·40
25	2·50	75	7·50	125	12·50	175	17·50	225	22·50	275	27·50	325	32·50	375	37·50	425	42·50	475	47·50
26	2·60	76	7·60	126	12·60	176	17·60	226	22·60	276	27·60	326	32·60	376	37·60	426	42·60	476	47·60
27	2·70	77	7·70	127	12·70	177	17·70	227	22·70	277	27·70	327	32·70	377	37·70	427	42·70	477	47·70
28	2·80	78	7·80	128	12·80	178	17·80	228	22·80	278	27·80	328	32·80	378	37·80	428	42·80	478	47·80
29	2·90	79	7·90	129	12·90	179	17·90	229	22·90	279	27·90	329	32·90	379	37·90	429	42·90	479	47·90
30	3·00	80	8·00	130	13·00	180	18·00	230	23·00	280	28·00	330	33·00	380	38·00	430	43·00	480	48·00
31	3·10	81	8·10	131	13·10	181	18·10	231	23·10	281	28·10	331	33·10	381	38·10	431	43·10	481	48·10
32	3·20	82	8·20	132	13·20	182	18·20	232	23·20	282	28·20	332	33·20	382	38·20	432	43·20	482	48·20
33	3·30	83	8·30	133	13·30	183	18·30	233	23·30	283	28·30	333	33·30	383	38·30	433	43·30	483	48·30
34	3·40	84	8·40	134	13·40	184	18·40	234	23·40	284	28·40	334	33·40	384	38·40	434	43·40	484	48·40
35	3·50	85	8·50	135	13·50	185	18·50	235	23·50	285	28·50	335	33·50	385	38·50	435	43·50	485	48·50
36	3·60	86	8·60	136	13·60	186	18·60	236	23·60	286	28·60	336	33·60	386	38·60	436	43·60	486	48·60
37	3·70	87	8·70	137	13·70	187	18·70	237	23·70	287	28·70	337	33·70	387	38·70	437	43·70	487	48·70
38	3·80	88	8·80	138	13·80	188	18·80	238	23·80	288	28·80	338	33·80	388	38·80	438	43·80	488	48·80
39	3·90	89	8·90	139	13·90	189	18·90	239	23·90	289	28·90	339	33·90	389	38·90	439	43·90	489	48·90
40	4·00	90	9·00	140	14·00	190	19·00	240	24·00	290	29·00	340	34·00	390	39·00	440	44·00	490	49·00
41	4·10	91	9·10	141	14·10	191	19·10	241	24·10	291	29·10	341	34·10	391	39·10	441	44·10	491	49·10
42	4·20	92	9·20	142	14·20	192	19·20	242	24·20	292	29·20	342	34·20	392	39·20	442	44·20	492	49·20
43	4·30	93	9·30	143	14·30	193	19·30	243	24·30	293	29·30	343	34·30	393	39·30	443	44·30	493	49·30
44	4·40	94	9·40	144	14·40	194	19·40	244	24·40	294	29·40	344	34·40	394	39·40	444	44·40	494	49·40
45	4·50	95	9·50	145	14·50	195	19·50	245	24·50	295	29·50	345	34·50	395	39·50	445	44·50	495	49·50
46	4·60	96	9·60	146	14·60	196	19·60	246	24·60	296	29·60	346	34·60	396	39·60	446	44·60	496	49·60
47	4·70	97	9·70	147	14·70	197	19·70	247	24·70	297	29·70	347	34·70	397	39·70	447	44·70	497	49·70
48	4·80	98	9·80	148	14·80	198	19·80	248	24·80	298	29·80	348	34·80	398	39·80	448	44·80	498	49·80
49	4·90	99	9·90	149	14·90	199	19·90	249	24·90	299	29·90	349	34·90	399	39·90	449	44·90	499	49·90
50	5·00	100	10·00	150	15·00	200	20·00	250	25·00	300	30·00	350	35·00	400	40·00	450	45·00	500	50·00
On Tax		**£1,000** £100		**£1,500** £150		**£2,000** £200		**£2,500** £250		**£3,000** £300		**£3,500** £350		**£4,000** £400		**£4,500** £450		**£5,000** £500	

For gains on residential property not eligible for private residence relief and carried interest.

Capital Gains Tax Rate for individuals 18%

£ or p	Tax £ or p	£ or p	Tax £ or p	£	Tax £	£	Tax £	£	Tax £	£	Tax £	£	Tax £	£	Tax £	£	Tax £	£	Tax £
1	0·18	51	9·18	101	18·18	151	27·18	201	36·18	251	45·18	301	54·18	351	63·18	401	72·18	451	81·18
2	0·36	52	9·36	102	18·36	152	27·36	202	36·36	252	45·36	302	54·36	352	63·36	402	72·36	452	81·36
3	0·54	53	9·54	103	18·54	153	27·54	203	36·54	253	45·54	303	54·54	353	63·54	403	72·54	453	81·54
4	0·72	54	9·72	104	18·72	154	27·72	204	36·72	254	45·72	304	54·72	354	63·72	404	72·72	454	81·72
5	0·90	55	9·90	105	18·90	155	27·90	205	36·90	255	45·90	305	54·90	355	63·90	405	72·90	455	81·90
6	1·08	56	10·08	106	19·08	156	28·08	206	37·08	256	46·08	306	55·08	356	64·08	406	73·08	456	82·08
7	1·26	57	10·26	107	19·26	157	28·26	207	37·26	257	46·26	307	55·26	357	64·26	407	73·26	457	82·26
8	1·44	58	10·44	108	19·44	158	28·44	208	37·44	258	46·44	308	55·44	358	64·44	408	73·44	458	82·44
9	1·62	59	10·62	109	19·62	159	28·62	209	37·62	259	46·62	309	55·62	359	64·62	409	73·62	459	82·62
10	1·80	60	10·80	110	19·80	160	28·80	210	37·80	260	46·80	310	55·80	360	64·80	410	73·80	460	82·80
11	1·98	61	10·98	111	19·98	161	28·98	211	37·98	261	46·98	311	55·98	361	64·98	411	73·98	461	82·98
12	2·16	62	11·16	112	20·16	162	29·16	212	38·16	262	47·16	312	56·16	362	65·16	412	74·16	462	83·16
13	2·34	63	11·34	113	20·34	163	29·34	213	38·34	263	47·34	313	56·34	363	65·34	413	74·34	463	83·34
14	2·52	64	11·52	114	20·52	164	29·52	214	38·52	264	47·52	314	56·52	364	65·52	414	74·52	464	83·52
15	2·70	65	11·70	115	20·70	165	29·70	215	38·70	265	47·70	315	56·70	365	65·70	415	74·70	465	83·70
16	2·88	66	11·88	116	20·88	166	29·88	216	38·88	266	47·88	316	56·88	366	65·88	416	74·88	466	83·88
17	3·06	67	12·06	117	21·06	167	30·06	217	39·06	267	48·06	317	57·06	367	66·06	417	75·06	467	84·06
18	3·24	68	12·24	118	21·24	168	30·24	218	39·24	268	48·24	318	57·24	368	66·24	418	75·24	468	84·24
19	3·42	69	12·42	119	21·42	169	30·42	219	39·42	269	48·42	319	57·42	369	66·42	419	75·42	469	84·42
20	3·60	70	12·60	120	21·60	170	30·60	220	39·60	270	48·60	320	57·60	370	66·60	420	75·60	470	84·60
21	3·78	71	12·78	121	21·78	171	30·78	221	39·78	271	48·78	321	57·78	371	66·78	421	75·78	471	84·78
22	3·96	72	12·96	122	21·96	172	30·96	222	39·96	272	48·96	322	57·96	372	66·96	422	75·96	472	84·96
23	4·14	73	13·14	123	22·14	173	31·14	223	40·14	273	49·14	323	58·14	373	67·14	423	76·14	473	85·14
24	4·32	74	13·32	124	22·32	174	31·32	224	40·32	274	49·32	324	58·32	374	67·32	424	76·32	474	85·32
25	4·50	75	13·50	125	22·50	175	31·50	225	40·50	275	49·50	325	58·50	375	67·50	425	76·50	475	85·50
26	4·68	76	13·68	126	22·68	176	31·68	226	40·68	276	49·68	326	58·68	376	67·68	426	76·68	476	85·68
27	4·86	77	13·86	127	22·86	177	31·86	227	40·86	277	49·86	327	58·86	377	67·86	427	76·86	477	85·86
28	5·04	78	14·04	128	23·04	178	32·04	228	41·04	278	50·04	328	59·04	378	68·04	428	77·04	478	86·04
29	5·22	79	14·22	129	23·22	179	32·22	229	41·22	279	50·22	329	59·22	379	68·22	429	77·22	479	86·22
30	5·40	80	14·40	130	23·40	180	32·40	230	41·40	280	50·40	330	59·40	380	68·40	430	77·40	480	86·40
31	5·58	81	14·58	131	23·58	181	32·58	231	41·58	281	50·58	331	59·58	381	68·58	431	77·58	481	86·58
32	5·76	82	14·76	132	23·76	182	32·76	232	41·76	282	50·76	332	59·76	382	68·76	432	77·76	482	86·76
33	5·94	83	14·94	133	23·94	183	32·94	233	41·94	283	50·94	333	59·94	383	68·94	433	77·94	483	86·94
34	6·12	84	15·12	134	24·12	184	33·12	234	42·12	284	51·12	334	60·12	384	69·12	434	78·12	484	87·12
35	6·30	85	15·30	135	24·30	185	33·30	235	42·30	285	51·30	335	60·30	385	69·30	435	78·30	485	87·30
36	6·48	86	15·48	136	24·48	186	33·48	236	42·48	286	51·48	336	60·48	386	69·48	436	78·48	486	87·48
37	6·66	87	15·66	137	24·66	187	33·66	237	42·66	287	51·66	337	60·66	387	69·66	437	78·66	487	87·66
38	6·84	88	15·84	138	24·84	188	33·84	238	42·84	288	51·84	338	60·84	388	69·84	438	78·84	488	87·84
39	7·02	89	16·02	139	25·02	189	34·02	239	43·02	289	52·02	339	61·02	389	70·02	439	79·02	489	88·02
40	7·20	90	16·20	140	25·20	190	34·20	240	43·20	290	52·20	340	61·20	390	70·20	440	79·20	490	88·20
41	7·38	91	16·38	141	25·38	191	34·38	241	43·38	291	52·38	341	61·38	391	70·38	441	79·38	491	88·38
42	7·56	92	16·56	142	25·56	192	34·56	242	43·56	292	52·56	342	61·56	392	70·56	442	79·56	492	88·56
43	7·74	93	16·74	143	25·74	193	34·74	243	43·74	293	52·74	343	61·74	393	70·74	443	79·74	493	88·74
44	7·92	94	16·92	144	25·92	194	34·92	244	43·92	294	52·92	344	61·92	394	70·92	444	79·92	494	88·92
45	8·10	95	17·10	145	26·10	195	35·10	245	44·10	295	53·10	345	62·10	395	71·10	445	80·10	495	89·10
46	8·28	96	17·28	146	26·28	196	35·28	246	44·28	296	53·28	346	62·28	396	71·28	446	80·28	496	89·28
47	8·46	97	17·46	147	26·46	197	35·46	247	44·46	297	53·46	347	62·46	397	71·46	447	80·46	497	89·46
48	8·64	98	17·64	148	26·64	198	35·64	248	44·64	298	53·64	348	62·64	398	71·64	448	80·64	498	89·64
49	8·82	99	17·82	149	26·82	199	35·82	249	44·82	299	53·82	349	62·82	399	71·82	449	80·82	499	89·82
50	9·00	100	18·00	150	27·00	200	36·00	250	45·00	300	54·00	350	63·00	400	72·00	450	81·00	500	90·00
On		£1,000		£1,500		£2,000		£2,500		£3,000		£3,500		£4,000		£4,500		£5,000	
Tax		£180		£270		£360		£450		£540		£630		£720		£810		£900	

19% Corporation Tax: Full Rate F.Y. 2018 and F.Y. 2019

£ or p	Tax £ or p	£ or p	Tax £ or p	£	Tax £	£	Tax £	£	Tax £	£	Tax £	£	Tax £	£	Tax £	£	Tax £	£	Tax £
1	0.19	**51**	9.69	**101**	19.19	**151**	28.69	**201**	38.19	**251**	47.69	**301**	57.19	**351**	66.69	**401**	76.19	**451**	85.69
2	0.38	**52**	9.88	**102**	19.38	**152**	28.88	**202**	38.38	**252**	47.88	**302**	57.38	**352**	66.88	**402**	76.38	**452**	85.88
3	0.57	**53**	10.07	**103**	19.57	**153**	29.07	**203**	38.57	**253**	48.07	**303**	57.57	**353**	67.07	**403**	76.57	**453**	86.07
4	0.76	**54**	10.26	**104**	19.76	**154**	29.26	**204**	38.76	**254**	48.26	**304**	57.76	**354**	67.26	**404**	76.76	**454**	86.26
5	0.95	**55**	10.45	**105**	19.95	**155**	29.45	**205**	38.95	**255**	48.45	**305**	57.95	**355**	67.45	**405**	76.95	**455**	86.45
6	1.14	**56**	10.64	**106**	20.14	**156**	29.64	**206**	39.14	**256**	48.64	**306**	58.14	**356**	67.64	**406**	77.14	**456**	86.64
7	1.33	**57**	10.83	**107**	20.33	**157**	29.83	**207**	39.33	**257**	48.83	**307**	58.33	**357**	67.83	**407**	77.33	**457**	86.83
8	1.52	**58**	11.02	**108**	20.52	**158**	30.02	**208**	39.52	**258**	49.02	**308**	58.52	**358**	68.02	**408**	77.52	**458**	87.02
9	1.71	**59**	11.21	**109**	20.71	**159**	30.21	**209**	39.71	**259**	49.21	**309**	58.71	**359**	68.21	**409**	77.71	**459**	87.21
10	1.90	**60**	11.40	**110**	20.90	**160**	30.40	**210**	39.90	**260**	49.40	**310**	58.90	**360**	68.40	**410**	77.90	**460**	87.40
11	2.09	**61**	11.59	**111**	21.09	**161**	30.59	**211**	40.09	**261**	49.59	**311**	59.09	**361**	68.59	**411**	78.09	**461**	87.59
12	2.28	**62**	11.78	**112**	21.28	**162**	30.78	**212**	40.28	**262**	49.78	**312**	59.28	**362**	68.78	**412**	78.28	**462**	87.78
13	2.47	**63**	11.97	**113**	21.47	**163**	30.97	**213**	40.47	**263**	49.97	**313**	59.47	**363**	68.97	**413**	78.47	**463**	87.97
14	2.66	**64**	12.16	**114**	21.66	**164**	31.16	**214**	40.66	**264**	50.16	**314**	59.66	**364**	69.16	**414**	78.66	**464**	88.16
15	2.85	**65**	12.35	**115**	21.85	**165**	31.35	**215**	40.85	**265**	50.35	**315**	59.85	**365**	69.35	**415**	78.85	**465**	88.35
16	3.04	**66**	12.54	**116**	22.04	**166**	31.54	**216**	41.04	**266**	50.54	**316**	60.04	**366**	69.54	**416**	79.04	**466**	88.54
17	3.23	**67**	12.73	**117**	22.23	**167**	31.73	**217**	41.23	**267**	50.73	**317**	60.23	**367**	69.73	**417**	79.23	**467**	88.73
18	3.42	**68**	12.92	**118**	22.42	**168**	31.92	**218**	41.42	**268**	50.92	**318**	60.42	**368**	69.92	**418**	79.42	**468**	88.92
19	3.61	**69**	13.11	**119**	22.61	**169**	32.11	**219**	41.61	**269**	51.11	**319**	60.61	**369**	70.11	**419**	79.61	**469**	89.11
20	3.80	**70**	13.30	**120**	22.80	**170**	32.30	**220**	41.80	**270**	51.30	**320**	60.80	**370**	70.30	**420**	79.80	**470**	89.30
21	3.99	**71**	13.49	**121**	22.99	**171**	32.49	**221**	41.99	**271**	51.49	**321**	60.99	**371**	70.49	**421**	79.99	**471**	89.49
22	4.18	**72**	13.68	**122**	23.18	**172**	32.68	**222**	42.18	**272**	51.68	**322**	61.18	**372**	70.68	**422**	80.18	**472**	89.68
23	4.37	**73**	13.87	**123**	23.37	**173**	32.87	**223**	42.37	**273**	51.87	**323**	61.37	**373**	70.87	**423**	80.37	**473**	89.87
24	4.56	**74**	14.06	**124**	23.56	**174**	33.06	**224**	42.56	**274**	52.06	**324**	61.56	**374**	71.06	**424**	80.56	**474**	90.06
25	4.75	**75**	14.25	**125**	23.75	**175**	33.25	**225**	42.75	**275**	52.25	**325**	61.75	**375**	71.25	**425**	80.75	**475**	90.25
26	4.94	**76**	14.44	**126**	23.94	**176**	33.44	**226**	42.94	**276**	52.44	**326**	61.94	**376**	71.44	**426**	80.94	**476**	90.44
27	5.13	**77**	14.63	**127**	24.13	**177**	33.63	**227**	43.13	**277**	52.63	**327**	62.13	**377**	71.63	**427**	81.13	**477**	90.63
28	5.32	**78**	14.82	**128**	24.32	**178**	33.82	**228**	43.32	**278**	52.82	**328**	62.32	**378**	71.82	**428**	81.32	**478**	90.82
29	5.51	**79**	15.01	**129**	24.51	**179**	34.01	**229**	43.51	**279**	53.01	**329**	62.51	**379**	72.01	**429**	81.51	**479**	91.01
30	5.70	**80**	15.20	**130**	24.70	**180**	34.20	**230**	43.70	**280**	53.20	**330**	62.70	**380**	72.20	**430**	81.70	**480**	91.20
31	5.89	**81**	15.39	**131**	24.89	**181**	34.39	**231**	43.89	**281**	53.39	**331**	62.89	**381**	72.39	**431**	81.89	**481**	91.39
32	6.08	**82**	15.58	**132**	25.08	**182**	34.58	**232**	44.08	**282**	53.58	**332**	63.08	**382**	72.58	**432**	82.08	**482**	91.58
33	6.27	**83**	15.77	**133**	25.27	**183**	34.77	**233**	44.27	**283**	53.77	**333**	63.27	**383**	72.77	**433**	82.27	**483**	91.77
34	6.46	**84**	15.96	**134**	25.46	**184**	34.96	**234**	44.46	**284**	53.96	**334**	63.46	**384**	72.96	**434**	82.46	**484**	91.96
35	6.65	**85**	16.15	**135**	25.65	**185**	35.15	**235**	44.65	**285**	54.15	**335**	63.65	**385**	73.15	**435**	82.65	**485**	92.15
36	6.84	**86**	16.34	**136**	25.84	**186**	35.34	**236**	44.84	**286**	54.34	**336**	63.84	**386**	73.34	**436**	82.84	**486**	92.34
37	7.03	**87**	16.53	**137**	26.03	**187**	35.53	**237**	45.03	**287**	54.53	**337**	64.03	**387**	73.53	**437**	83.03	**487**	92.53
38	7.22	**88**	16.72	**138**	26.22	**188**	35.72	**238**	45.22	**288**	54.72	**338**	64.22	**388**	73.72	**438**	83.22	**488**	92.72
39	7.41	**89**	16.91	**139**	26.41	**189**	35.91	**239**	45.41	**289**	54.91	**339**	64.41	**389**	73.91	**439**	83.41	**489**	92.91
40	7.60	**90**	17.10	**140**	26.60	**190**	36.10	**240**	45.60	**290**	55.10	**340**	64.60	**390**	74.10	**440**	83.60	**490**	93.10
41	7.79	**91**	17.29	**141**	26.79	**191**	36.29	**241**	45.79	**291**	55.29	**341**	64.79	**391**	74.29	**441**	83.79	**491**	93.29
42	7.98	**92**	17.48	**142**	26.98	**192**	36.48	**242**	45.98	**292**	55.48	**342**	64.98	**392**	74.48	**442**	83.98	**492**	93.48
43	8.17	**93**	17.67	**143**	27.17	**193**	36.67	**243**	46.17	**293**	55.67	**343**	65.17	**393**	74.67	**443**	84.17	**493**	93.67
44	8.36	**94**	17.86	**144**	27.36	**194**	36.86	**244**	46.36	**294**	55.86	**344**	65.36	**394**	74.86	**444**	84.36	**494**	93.86
45	8.55	**95**	18.05	**145**	27.55	**195**	37.05	**245**	46.55	**295**	56.05	**345**	65.55	**395**	75.05	**445**	84.55	**495**	94.05
46	8.74	**96**	18.24	**146**	27.74	**196**	37.24	**246**	46.74	**296**	56.24	**346**	65.74	**396**	75.24	**446**	84.74	**496**	94.24
47	8.93	**97**	18.43	**147**	27.93	**197**	37.43	**247**	46.93	**297**	56.43	**347**	65.93	**397**	75.43	**447**	84.93	**497**	94.43
48	9.12	**98**	18.62	**148**	28.12	**198**	37.62	**248**	47.12	**298**	56.62	**348**	66.12	**398**	75.62	**448**	85.12	**498**	94.62
49	9.31	**99**	18.81	**149**	28.31	**199**	37.81	**249**	47.31	**299**	56.81	**349**	66.31	**399**	75.81	**449**	85.31	**499**	94.81
50	9.50	**100**	19.00	**150**	28.50	**200**	38.00	**250**	47.50	**300**	57.00	**350**	66.50	**400**	76.00	**450**	85.50	**500**	95.00
On Tax		**£1,000** £190		**£1,500** £285		**£2,000** £380		**£2,500** £475		**£3,000** £570		**£3,500** £665		**£4,000** £760		**£4,500** £855		**£5,000** £950	

(a) Payable on savings and non-savings income (if 0% band exceeded) up to £34,500.
For 2019/20, payable on savings and non-savings income (if 0% band exceeded) up to £37,500.

Basic Rate 2018/19 and 2019/20 Income Tax (a) 20% and main Capital Gains Tax for higher rate taxpayers, and trustees and personal representatives (b)

£ or p	Tax £ or p	£ or p	Tax £ or p	£	Tax £	£	Tax £	£	Tax £	£	Tax £	£	Tax £	£	Tax £	£	Tax £	£	Tax £
1	0·20	**51**	10·20	**101**	20·20	**151**	30·20	**201**	40·20	**251**	50·20	**301**	60·20	**351**	70·20	**401**	80·20	**451**	90·20
2	0·40	**52**	10·40	**102**	20·40	**152**	30·40	**202**	40·40	**252**	50·40	**302**	60·40	**352**	70·40	**402**	80·40	**452**	90·40
3	0·60	**53**	10·60	**103**	20·60	**153**	30·60	**203**	40·60	**253**	50·60	**303**	60·60	**353**	70·60	**403**	80·60	**453**	90·60
4	0·80	**54**	10·80	**104**	20·80	**154**	30·80	**204**	40·80	**254**	50·80	**304**	60·80	**354**	70·80	**404**	80·80	**454**	90·80
5	1·00	**55**	11·00	**105**	21·00	**155**	31·00	**205**	41·00	**255**	51·00	**305**	61·00	**355**	71·00	**405**	81·00	**455**	91·00
6	1·20	**56**	11·20	**106**	21·20	**156**	31·20	**206**	41·20	**256**	51·20	**306**	61·20	**356**	71·20	**406**	81·20	**456**	91·20
7	1·40	**57**	11·40	**107**	21·40	**157**	31·40	**207**	41·40	**257**	51·40	**307**	61·40	**357**	71·40	**407**	81·40	**457**	91·40
8	1·60	**58**	11·60	**108**	21·60	**158**	31·60	**208**	41·60	**258**	51·60	**308**	61·60	**358**	71·60	**408**	81·60	**458**	91·60
9	1·80	**59**	11·80	**109**	21·80	**159**	31·80	**209**	41·80	**259**	51·80	**309**	61·80	**359**	71·80	**409**	81·80	**459**	91·80
10	2·00	**60**	12·00	**110**	22·00	**160**	32·00	**210**	42·00	**260**	52·00	**310**	62·00	**360**	72·00	**410**	82·00	**460**	92·00
11	2·20	**61**	12·20	**111**	22·20	**161**	32·20	**211**	42·20	**261**	52·20	**311**	62·20	**361**	72·20	**411**	82·20	**461**	92·20
12	2·40	**62**	12·40	**112**	22·40	**162**	32·40	**212**	42·40	**262**	52·40	**312**	62·40	**362**	72·40	**412**	82·40	**462**	92·40
13	2·60	**63**	12·60	**113**	22·60	**163**	32·60	**213**	42·60	**263**	52·60	**313**	62·60	**363**	72·60	**413**	82·60	**463**	92·60
14	2·80	**64**	12·80	**114**	22·80	**164**	32·80	**214**	42·80	**264**	52·80	**314**	62·80	**364**	72·80	**414**	82·80	**464**	92·80
15	3·00	**65**	13·00	**115**	23·00	**165**	33·00	**215**	43·00	**265**	53·00	**315**	63·00	**365**	73·00	**415**	83·00	**465**	93·00
16	3·20	**66**	13·20	**116**	23·20	**166**	33·20	**216**	43·20	**266**	53·20	**316**	63·20	**366**	73·20	**416**	83·20	**466**	93·20
17	3·40	**67**	13·40	**117**	23·40	**167**	33·40	**217**	43·40	**267**	53·40	**317**	63·40	**367**	73·40	**417**	83·40	**467**	93·40
18	3·60	**68**	13·60	**118**	23·60	**168**	33·60	**218**	43·60	**268**	53·60	**318**	63·60	**368**	73·60	**418**	83·60	**468**	93·60
19	3·80	**69**	13·80	**119**	23·80	**169**	33·80	**219**	43·80	**269**	53·80	**319**	63·80	**369**	73·80	**419**	83·80	**469**	93·80
20	4·00	**70**	14·00	**120**	24·00	**170**	34·00	**220**	44·00	**270**	54·00	**320**	64·00	**370**	74·00	**420**	84·00	**470**	94·00
21	4·20	**71**	14·20	**121**	24·20	**171**	34·20	**221**	44·20	**271**	54·20	**321**	64·20	**371**	74·20	**421**	84·20	**471**	94·20
22	4·40	**72**	14·40	**122**	24·40	**172**	34·40	**222**	44·40	**272**	54·40	**322**	64·40	**372**	74·40	**422**	84·40	**472**	94·40
23	4·60	**73**	14·60	**123**	24·60	**173**	34·60	**223**	44·60	**273**	54·60	**323**	64·60	**373**	74·60	**423**	84·60	**473**	94·60
24	4·80	**74**	14·80	**124**	24·80	**174**	34·80	**224**	44·80	**274**	54·80	**324**	64·80	**374**	74·80	**424**	84·80	**474**	94·80
25	5·00	**75**	15·00	**125**	25·00	**175**	35·00	**225**	45·00	**275**	55·00	**325**	65·00	**375**	75·00	**425**	85·00	**475**	95·00
26	5·20	**76**	15·20	**126**	25·20	**176**	35·20	**226**	45·20	**276**	55·20	**326**	65·20	**376**	75·20	**426**	85·20	**476**	95·20
27	5·40	**77**	15·40	**127**	25·40	**177**	35·40	**227**	45·40	**277**	55·40	**327**	65·40	**377**	75·40	**427**	85·40	**477**	95·40
28	5·60	**78**	15·60	**128**	25·60	**178**	35·60	**228**	45·60	**278**	55·60	**328**	65·60	**378**	75·60	**428**	85·60	**478**	95·60
29	5·80	**79**	15·80	**129**	25·80	**179**	35·80	**229**	45·80	**279**	55·80	**329**	65·80	**379**	75·80	**429**	85·80	**479**	95·80
30	6·00	**80**	16·00	**130**	26·00	**180**	36·00	**230**	46·00	**280**	56·00	**330**	66·00	**380**	76·00	**430**	86·00	**480**	96·00
31	6·20	**81**	16·20	**131**	26·20	**181**	36·20	**231**	46·20	**281**	56·20	**331**	66·20	**381**	76·20	**431**	86·20	**481**	96·20
32	6·40	**82**	16·40	**132**	26·40	**182**	36·40	**232**	46·40	**282**	56·40	**332**	66·40	**382**	76·40	**432**	86·40	**482**	96·40
33	6·60	**83**	16·60	**133**	26·60	**183**	36·60	**233**	46·60	**283**	56·60	**333**	66·60	**383**	76·60	**433**	86·60	**483**	96·60
34	6·80	**84**	16·80	**134**	26·80	**184**	36·80	**234**	46·80	**284**	56·80	**334**	66·80	**384**	76·80	**434**	86·80	**484**	96·80
35	7·00	**85**	17·00	**135**	27·00	**185**	37·00	**235**	47·00	**285**	57·00	**335**	67·00	**385**	77·00	**435**	87·00	**485**	97·00
36	7·20	**86**	17·20	**136**	27·20	**186**	37·20	**236**	47·20	**286**	57·20	**336**	67·20	**386**	77·20	**436**	87·20	**486**	97·20
37	7·40	**87**	17·40	**137**	27·40	**187**	37·40	**237**	47·40	**287**	57·40	**337**	67·40	**387**	77·40	**437**	87·40	**487**	97·40
38	7·60	**88**	17·60	**138**	27·60	**188**	37·60	**238**	47·60	**288**	57·60	**338**	67·60	**388**	77·60	**438**	87·60	**488**	97·60
39	7·80	**89**	17·80	**139**	27·80	**189**	37·80	**239**	47·80	**289**	57·80	**339**	67·80	**389**	77·80	**439**	87·80	**489**	97·80
40	8·00	**90**	18·00	**140**	28·00	**190**	38·00	**240**	48·00	**290**	58·00	**340**	68·00	**390**	78·00	**440**	88·00	**490**	98·00
41	8·20	**91**	18·20	**141**	28·20	**191**	38·20	**241**	48·20	**291**	58·20	**341**	68·20	**391**	78·20	**441**	88·20	**491**	98·20
42	8·40	**92**	18·40	**142**	28·40	**192**	38·40	**242**	48·40	**292**	58·40	**342**	68·40	**392**	78·40	**442**	88·40	**492**	98·40
43	8·60	**93**	18·60	**143**	28·60	**193**	38·60	**243**	48·60	**293**	58·60	**343**	68·60	**393**	78·60	**443**	88·60	**493**	98·60
44	8·80	**94**	18·80	**144**	28·80	**194**	38·80	**244**	48·80	**294**	58·80	**344**	68·80	**394**	78·80	**444**	88·80	**494**	98·80
45	9·00	**95**	19·00	**145**	29·00	**195**	39·00	**245**	49·00	**295**	59·00	**345**	69·00	**395**	79·00	**445**	89·00	**495**	99·00
46	9·20	**96**	19·20	**146**	29·20	**196**	39·20	**246**	49·20	**296**	59·20	**346**	69·20	**396**	79·20	**446**	89·20	**496**	99·20
47	9·40	**97**	19·40	**147**	29·40	**197**	39·40	**247**	49·40	**297**	59·40	**347**	69·40	**397**	79·40	**447**	89·40	**497**	99·40
48	9·60	**98**	19·60	**148**	29·60	**198**	39·60	**248**	49·60	**298**	59·60	**348**	69·60	**398**	79·60	**448**	89·60	**498**	99·60
49	9·80	**99**	19·80	**149**	29·80	**199**	39·80	**249**	49·80	**299**	59·80	**349**	69·80	**399**	79·80	**449**	89·80	**499**	99·80
50	10·00	**100**	20·00	**150**	30·00	**200**	40·00	**250**	50·00	**300**	60·00	**350**	70·00	**400**	80·00	**450**	90·00	**500**	100·00
On		**£1,000**		**£1,500**		**£2,000**		**£2,500**		**£3,000**		**£3,500**		**£4,000**		**£4,500**		**£5,000**	
Tax		£200		£300		£400		£500		£600		£700		£800		£900		£1,000	

28% Higher Rate Capital Gains Tax Rate for individuals

For gains on residential property not eligible for private residence relief, and carried interest, and rate for trustees and personal representatives for gains on residential property not eligible for private residence relief.

£ or p	Tax £ or p	£ or p	Tax £ or p	£	Tax £	£	Tax £	£	Tax £	£	Tax £	£	Tax £	£	Tax £	£	Tax £	£	Tax £
1	0·28	**51**	14·28	**101**	28·28	**151**	42·28	**201**	56·28	**251**	70·28	**301**	84·28	**351**	8·28	**401**	112·28	**451**	126·28
2	0·56	**52**	14·56	**102**	28·56	**152**	42·56	**202**	56·56	**252**	70·56	**302**	84·56	**352**	8·56	**402**	112·56	**452**	126·56
3	0·84	**53**	14·84	**103**	28·84	**153**	42·84	**203**	56·84	**253**	70·84	**303**	84·84	**353**	8·84	**403**	112·84	**453**	126·84
4	1·12	**54**	15·12	**104**	29·12	**154**	43·12	**204**	57·12	**254**	71·12	**304**	85·12	**354**	9·12	**404**	113·12	**454**	127·12
5	1·40	**55**	15·40	**105**	29·40	**155**	43·40	**205**	57·40	**255**	71·40	**305**	85·40	**355**	9·40	**405**	113·40	**455**	127·40
6	1·68	**56**	15·68	**106**	29·68	**156**	43·68	**206**	57·68	**256**	71·68	**306**	85·68	**356**	9·68	**406**	113·68	**456**	127·68
7	1·96	**57**	15·96	**107**	29·96	**157**	43·96	**207**	57·96	**257**	71·96	**307**	85·96	**357**	9·96	**407**	113·96	**457**	127·96
8	2·24	**58**	16·24	**108**	30·24	**158**	44·24	**208**	58·24	**258**	72·24	**308**	86·24	**358**	100·24	**408**	114·24	**458**	128·24
9	2·52	**59**	16·52	**109**	30·52	**159**	44·52	**209**	58·52	**259**	72·52	**309**	86·52	**359**	100·52	**409**	114·52	**459**	128·52
10	2·80	**60**	16·80	**110**	30·80	**160**	44·80	**210**	58·80	**260**	72·80	**310**	86·80	**360**	100·80	**410**	114·80	**460**	128·80
11	3·08	**61**	17·08	**111**	31·08	**161**	45·08	**211**	59·08	**261**	73·08	**311**	87·08	**361**	101·08	**411**	115·08	**461**	129·08
12	3·36	**62**	17·36	**112**	31·36	**162**	45·36	**212**	59·36	**262**	73·36	**312**	87·36	**362**	101·36	**412**	115·36	**462**	129·36
13	3·64	**63**	17·64	**113**	31·64	**163**	45·64	**213**	59·64	**263**	73·64	**313**	87·64	**363**	101·64	**413**	115·64	**463**	129·64
14	3·92	**64**	17·92	**114**	31·92	**164**	45·92	**214**	59·92	**264**	73·92	**314**	87·92	**364**	101·92	**414**	115·92	**464**	129·92
15	4·20	**65**	18·20	**115**	32·20	**165**	46·20	**215**	60·20	**265**	74·20	**315**	88·20	**365**	102·20	**415**	116·20	**465**	130·20
16	4·48	**66**	18·48	**116**	32·48	**166**	46·48	**216**	60·48	**266**	74·48	**316**	88·48	**366**	102·48	**416**	116·48	**466**	130·48
17	4·76	**67**	18·76	**117**	32·76	**167**	46·76	**217**	60·76	**267**	74·76	**317**	88·76	**367**	102·76	**417**	116·76	**467**	130·76
18	5·04	**68**	19·04	**118**	33·04	**168**	47·04	**218**	61·04	**268**	75·04	**318**	89·04	**368**	103·04	**418**	117·04	**468**	131·04
19	5·32	**69**	19·32	**119**	33·32	**169**	47·32	**219**	61·32	**269**	75·32	**319**	89·32	**369**	103·32	**419**	117·32	**469**	131·32
20	5·60	**70**	19·60	**120**	33·60	**170**	47·60	**220**	61·60	**270**	75·60	**320**	89·60	**370**	103·60	**420**	117·60	**470**	131·60
21	5·88	**71**	19·88	**121**	33·88	**171**	47·88	**221**	61·88	**271**	75·88	**321**	89·88	**371**	103·88	**421**	117·88	**471**	131·88
22	6·16	**72**	20·16	**122**	34·16	**172**	48·16	**222**	62·16	**272**	76·16	**322**	90·16	**372**	104·16	**422**	118·16	**472**	132·16
23	6·44	**73**	20·44	**123**	34·44	**173**	48·44	**223**	62·44	**273**	76·44	**323**	90·44	**373**	104·44	**423**	118·44	**473**	132·44
24	6·72	**74**	20·72	**124**	34·72	**174**	48·72	**224**	62·72	**274**	76·72	**324**	90·72	**374**	104·72	**424**	118·72	**474**	132·72
25	7·00	**75**	21·00	**125**	35·00	**175**	49·00	**225**	63·00	**275**	77·00	**325**	91·00	**375**	105·00	**425**	119·00	**475**	133·00
26	7·28	**76**	21·28	**126**	35·28	**176**	49·28	**226**	63·28	**276**	77·28	**326**	91·28	**376**	105·28	**426**	119·28	**476**	133·28
27	7·56	**77**	21·56	**127**	35·56	**177**	49·56	**227**	63·56	**277**	77·56	**327**	91·56	**377**	105·56	**427**	119·56	**477**	133·56
28	7·84	**78**	21·84	**128**	35·84	**178**	49·84	**228**	63·84	**278**	77·84	**328**	91·84	**378**	105·84	**428**	119·84	**478**	133·84
29	8·12	**79**	22·12	**129**	36·12	**179**	50·12	**229**	64·12	**279**	78·12	**329**	92·12	**379**	106·12	**429**	120·12	**479**	134·12
30	8·40	**80**	22·40	**130**	36·40	**180**	50·40	**230**	64·40	**280**	78·40	**330**	92·40	**380**	106·40	**430**	120·40	**480**	134·40
31	8·68	**81**	22·68	**131**	36·68	**181**	50·68	**231**	64·68	**281**	78·68	**331**	92·68	**381**	106·68	**431**	120·68	**481**	134·68
32	8·96	**82**	22·96	**132**	36·96	**182**	50·96	**232**	64·96	**282**	78·96	**332**	92·96	**382**	106·96	**432**	120·96	**482**	134·96
33	9·24	**83**	23·24	**133**	37·24	**183**	51·24	**233**	65·24	**283**	79·24	**333**	93·24	**383**	107·24	**433**	121·24	**483**	135·24
34	9·52	**84**	23·52	**134**	37·52	**184**	51·52	**234**	65·52	**284**	79·52	**334**	93·52	**384**	107·52	**434**	121·52	**484**	135·52
35	9·80	**85**	23·80	**135**	37·80	**185**	51·80	**235**	65·80	**285**	79·80	**335**	93·80	**385**	107·80	**435**	121·80	**485**	135·80
36	10·08	**86**	24·08	**136**	38·08	**186**	52·08	**236**	66·08	**286**	80·08	**336**	94·08	**386**	108·08	**436**	122·08	**486**	136·08
37	10·36	**87**	24·36	**137**	38·36	**187**	52·36	**237**	66·36	**287**	80·36	**337**	94·36	**387**	108·36	**437**	122·36	**487**	136·36
38	10·64	**88**	24·64	**138**	38·64	**188**	52·64	**238**	66·64	**288**	80·64	**338**	94·64	**388**	108·64	**438**	122·64	**488**	136·64
39	10·92	**89**	24·92	**139**	38·92	**189**	52·92	**239**	66·92	**289**	80·92	**339**	94·92	**389**	108·92	**439**	122·92	**489**	136·92
40	11·20	**90**	25·20	**140**	39·20	**190**	53·20	**240**	67·20	**290**	81·20	**340**	95·20	**390**	109·20	**440**	123·20	**490**	137·20
41	11·48	**91**	25·48	**141**	39·48	**191**	53·48	**241**	67·48	**291**	81·48	**341**	95·48	**391**	109·48	**441**	123·48	**491**	137·48
42	11·76	**92**	25·76	**142**	39·76	**192**	53·76	**242**	67·76	**292**	81·76	**342**	95·76	**392**	109·76	**442**	123·76	**492**	137·76
43	12·04	**93**	26·04	**143**	40·04	**193**	54·04	**243**	68·04	**293**	82·04	**343**	96·04	**393**	110·04	**443**	124·04	**493**	138·04
44	12·32	**94**	26·32	**144**	40·32	**194**	54·32	**244**	68·32	**294**	82·32	**344**	96·32	**394**	110·32	**444**	124·32	**494**	138·32
45	12·60	**95**	26·60	**145**	40·60	**195**	54·60	**245**	68·60	**295**	82·60	**345**	96·60	**395**	110·60	**445**	124·60	**495**	138·60
46	12·88	**96**	26·88	**146**	40·88	**196**	54·88	**246**	68·88	**296**	82·88	**346**	96·88	**396**	110·88	**446**	124·88	**496**	138·88
47	13·16	**97**	27·16	**147**	41·16	**197**	55·16	**247**	69·16	**297**	83·16	**347**	97·16	**397**	111·16	**447**	125·16	**497**	139·16
48	13·44	**98**	27·44	**148**	41·44	**198**	55·44	**248**	69·44	**298**	83·44	**348**	97·44	**398**	111·44	**448**	125·44	**498**	139·44
49	13·72	**99**	27·72	**149**	41·72	**199**	55·72	**249**	69·72	**299**	83·72	**349**	97·72	**399**	111·72	**449**	125·72	**499**	139·72
50	14·00	**100**	28·00	**150**	42·00	**200**	56·00	**250**	70·00	**300**	84·00	**350**	98·00	**400**	112·00	**450**	126·00	**500**	140·00

On	**£1,000**	**£1,500**	**£2,000**	**£2,500**	**£3,000**	**£3,500**	**£4,000**	**£4,500**	**£5,000**
Tax	£280	£420	£560	£700	£840	£980	£1,120	£1,260	£1,400

Payable by higher rate taxpayers on dividends exceeding the dividend allowance. (Note: The dividend allowance has been reduced from £5,000 to £2,000 for 2018/19 onwards).

2018/19 and 2019/20: Income Tax on Dividend Income 32·5%

£ or p	Tax £ or p	£ or p	Tax £ or p	£	Tax £	£	Tax £	£	Tax £	£	Tax £	£	Tax £	£	Tax £	£	Tax £	£	Tax £
1	0·33	**51**	16·58	**101**	32·83	**151**	49·08	**201**	65·33	**251**	81·58	**301**	97·83	**351**	114·08	**401**	130·33	**451**	146·58
2	0·65	**52**	16·90	**102**	33·15	**152**	49·40	**202**	65·65	**252**	81·90	**302**	98·15	**352**	114·40	**402**	130·65	**452**	146·90
3	0·98	**53**	17·23	**103**	33·48	**153**	49·73	**203**	65·98	**253**	82·23	**303**	98·48	**353**	114·73	**403**	130·98	**453**	147·23
4	1·30	**54**	17·55	**104**	33·80	**154**	50·05	**204**	66·30	**254**	82·55	**304**	98·80	**354**	115·05	**404**	131·30	**454**	147·55
5	1·63	**55**	17·88	**105**	34·13	**155**	50·38	**205**	66·63	**255**	82·88	**305**	99·13	**355**	115·38	**405**	131·63	**455**	147·88
6	1·95	**56**	18·20	**106**	34·45	**156**	50·70	**206**	66·95	**256**	83·20	**306**	99·45	**356**	115·70	**406**	131·95	**456**	148·20
7	2·28	**57**	18·53	**107**	34·78	**157**	51·03	**207**	67·28	**257**	83·53	**307**	99·78	**357**	116·03	**407**	132·28	**457**	148·53
8	2·60	**58**	18·85	**108**	35·10	**158**	51·35	**208**	67·60	**258**	83·85	**308**	100·10	**358**	116·35	**408**	132·60	**458**	148·85
9	2·93	**59**	19·18	**109**	35·43	**159**	51·68	**209**	67·93	**259**	84·18	**309**	100·43	**359**	116·68	**409**	132·93	**459**	149·18
10	3·25	**60**	19·50	**110**	35·75	**160**	52·00	**210**	68·25	**260**	84·50	**310**	100·75	**360**	117·00	**410**	133·25	**460**	149·50
11	3·58	**61**	19·83	**111**	36·08	**161**	52·33	**211**	68·58	**261**	84·83	**311**	101·08	**361**	117·33	**411**	133·58	**461**	149·83
12	3·90	**62**	20·15	**112**	36·40	**162**	52·65	**212**	68·90	**262**	85·15	**312**	101·40	**362**	117·65	**412**	133·90	**462**	150·15
13	4·23	**63**	20·48	**113**	36·73	**163**	52·98	**213**	69·23	**263**	85·48	**313**	101·73	**363**	117·98	**413**	134·23	**463**	150·48
14	4·55	**64**	20·80	**114**	37·05	**164**	53·30	**214**	69·55	**264**	85·80	**314**	102·05	**364**	118·30	**414**	134·55	**464**	150·80
15	4·88	**65**	21·13	**115**	37·38	**165**	53·63	**215**	69·88	**265**	86·13	**315**	102·38	**365**	118·63	**415**	134·88	**465**	151·13
16	5·20	**66**	21·45	**116**	37·70	**166**	53·95	**216**	70·20	**266**	86·45	**316**	102·70	**366**	118·95	**416**	135·20	**466**	151·45
17	5·53	**67**	21·78	**117**	38·03	**167**	54·28	**217**	70·53	**267**	86·78	**317**	103·03	**367**	119·28	**417**	135·53	**467**	151·78
18	5·85	**68**	22·10	**118**	38·35	**168**	54·60	**218**	70·85	**268**	87·10	**318**	103·35	**368**	119·60	**418**	135·85	**468**	152·10
19	6·18	**69**	22·43	**119**	38·68	**169**	54·93	**219**	71·18	**269**	87·43	**319**	103·68	**369**	119·93	**419**	136·18	**469**	152·43
20	6·50	**70**	22·75	**120**	39·00	**170**	55·25	**220**	71·50	**270**	87·75	**320**	104·00	**370**	120·25	**420**	136·50	**470**	152·75
21	6·83	**71**	23·08	**121**	39·33	**171**	55·58	**221**	71·83	**271**	88·08	**321**	104·33	**371**	120·58	**421**	136·83	**471**	153·08
22	7·15	**72**	23·40	**122**	39·65	**172**	55·90	**222**	72·15	**272**	88·40	**322**	104·65	**372**	120·90	**422**	137·15	**472**	153·40
23	7·48	**73**	23·73	**123**	39·98	**173**	56·23	**223**	72·48	**273**	88·73	**323**	104·98	**373**	121·23	**423**	137·48	**473**	153·73
24	7·80	**74**	24·05	**124**	40·30	**174**	56·55	**224**	72·80	**274**	89·05	**324**	105·30	**374**	121·55	**424**	137·80	**474**	154·05
25	8·13	**75**	24·38	**125**	40·63	**175**	56·88	**225**	73·13	**275**	89·38	**325**	105·63	**375**	121·88	**425**	138·13	**475**	154·38
26	8·45	**76**	24·70	**126**	40·95	**176**	57·20	**226**	73·45	**276**	89·70	**326**	105·95	**376**	122·20	**426**	138·45	**476**	154·70
27	8·78	**77**	25·03	**127**	41·28	**177**	57·53	**227**	73·78	**277**	90·03	**327**	106·28	**377**	122·53	**427**	138·78	**477**	155·03
28	9·10	**78**	25·35	**128**	41·60	**178**	57·85	**228**	74·10	**278**	90·35	**328**	106·60	**378**	122·85	**428**	139·10	**478**	155·35
29	9·43	**79**	25·68	**129**	41·93	**179**	58·18	**229**	74·43	**279**	90·68	**329**	106·93	**379**	123·18	**429**	139·43	**479**	155·68
30	9·75	**80**	26·00	**130**	42·25	**180**	58·50	**230**	74·75	**280**	91·00	**330**	107·25	**380**	123·50	**430**	139·75	**480**	156·00
31	10·08	**81**	26·33	**131**	42·58	**181**	58·83	**231**	75·08	**281**	91·33	**331**	107·58	**381**	123·83	**431**	140·08	**481**	156·33
32	10·40	**82**	26·65	**132**	42·90	**182**	59·15	**232**	75·40	**282**	91·65	**332**	107·90	**382**	124·15	**432**	140·40	**482**	156·65
33	10·73	**83**	26·98	**133**	43·23	**183**	59·48	**233**	75·73	**283**	91·98	**333**	108·23	**383**	124·48	**433**	140·73	**483**	156·98
34	11·05	**84**	27·30	**134**	43·55	**184**	59·80	**234**	76·05	**284**	92·30	**334**	108·55	**384**	124·80	**434**	141·05	**484**	157·30
35	11·38	**85**	27·63	**135**	43·88	**185**	60·13	**235**	76·38	**285**	92·63	**335**	108·88	**385**	125·13	**435**	141·38	**485**	157·63
36	11·70	**86**	27·95	**136**	44·20	**186**	60·45	**236**	76·70	**286**	92·95	**336**	109·20	**386**	125·45	**436**	141·70	**486**	157·95
37	12·03	**87**	28·28	**137**	44·53	**187**	60·78	**237**	77·03	**287**	93·28	**337**	109·53	**387**	125·78	**437**	142·03	**487**	158·28
38	12·35	**88**	28·60	**138**	44·85	**188**	61·10	**238**	77·35	**288**	93·60	**338**	109·85	**388**	126·10	**438**	142·35	**488**	158·60
39	12·68	**89**	28·93	**139**	45·18	**189**	61·43	**239**	77·68	**289**	93·93	**339**	110·18	**389**	126·43	**439**	142·68	**489**	158·93
40	13·00	**90**	29·25	**140**	45·50	**190**	61·75	**240**	78·00	**290**	94·25	**340**	110·50	**390**	126·75	**440**	143·00	**490**	159·25
41	13·33	**91**	29·58	**141**	45·83	**191**	62·08	**241**	78·33	**291**	94·58	**341**	110·83	**391**	127·08	**441**	143·33	**491**	159·58
42	13·65	**92**	29·90	**142**	46·15	**192**	62·40	**242**	78·65	**292**	94·90	**342**	111·15	**392**	127·40	**442**	143·65	**492**	159·90
43	13·98	**93**	30·23	**143**	46·48	**193**	62·73	**243**	78·98	**293**	95·23	**343**	111·48	**393**	127·73	**443**	143·98	**493**	160·23
44	14·30	**94**	30·55	**144**	46·80	**194**	63·05	**244**	79·30	**294**	95·55	**344**	111·80	**394**	128·05	**444**	144·30	**494**	160·55
45	14·63	**95**	30·88	**145**	47·13	**195**	63·38	**245**	79·63	**295**	95·88	**345**	112·13	**395**	128·38	**445**	144·63	**495**	160·88
46	14·95	**96**	31·20	**146**	47·45	**196**	63·70	**246**	79·95	**296**	96·20	**346**	112·45	**396**	128·70	**446**	144·95	**496**	161·20
47	15·28	**97**	31·53	**147**	47·78	**197**	64·03	**247**	80·28	**297**	96·53	**347**	112·78	**397**	129·03	**447**	145·28	**497**	161·53
48	15·60	**98**	31·85	**148**	48·10	**198**	64·35	**248**	80·60	**298**	96·85	**348**	113·10	**398**	129·35	**448**	145·60	**498**	161·85
49	15·93	**99**	32·18	**149**	48·43	**199**	64·68	**249**	80·93	**299**	97·18	**349**	113·43	**399**	129·68	**449**	145·93	**499**	162·18
50	16·25	**100**	32·50	**150**	48·75	**200**	65·00	**250**	81·25	**300**	97·50	**350**	113·75	**400**	130·00	**450**	146·25	**500**	162·50
On	Tax	**£1,000**	£325	**£1,500**	£488	**£2,000**	£650	**£2,500**	£813	**£3,000**	£975	**£3,500**	£1,138	**£4,000**	£1,300	**£4,500**	£1,463	**£5,000**	£1,625

32·5% 2018/19 and 2019/20: Income Tax on Dividend Income

Payable by higher rate taxpayers on dividends exceeding the dividend allowance.
(Note: The dividend allowance has been reduced from £5,000 to £2,000 for 2018/19 onwards).

£ or p	Tax £ or p	£ or p	Tax £ or p	£	Tax £	£	Tax £	£	Tax £	£	Tax £	£	Tax £	£	Tax £	£	Tax £	£	Tax £
501	162·83	**551**	179·08	**601**	195·33	**651**	211·58	**701**	227·83	**751**	244·08	**801**	260·33	**851**	276·58	**901**	292·83	**951**	309·08
502	163·15	**552**	179·40	**602**	195·65	**652**	211·90	**702**	228·15	**752**	244·40	**802**	260·65	**852**	276·90	**902**	293·15	**952**	309·40
503	163·48	**553**	179·73	**603**	195·98	**653**	212·23	**703**	228·48	**753**	244·73	**803**	260·98	**853**	277·23	**903**	293·48	**953**	309·73
504	163·80	**554**	180·05	**604**	196·30	**654**	212·55	**704**	228·80	**754**	245·05	**804**	261·30	**854**	277·55	**904**	293·80	**954**	310·05
505	164·13	**555**	180·38	**605**	196·63	**655**	212·88	**705**	229·13	**755**	245·38	**805**	261·63	**855**	277·88	**905**	294·13	**955**	310·38
506	164·45	**556**	180·70	**606**	196·95	**656**	213·20	**706**	229·45	**756**	245·70	**806**	261·95	**856**	278·20	**906**	294·45	**956**	310·70
507	164·78	**557**	181·03	**607**	197·28	**657**	213·53	**707**	229·78	**757**	246·03	**807**	262·28	**857**	278·53	**907**	294·78	**957**	311·03
508	165·10	**558**	181·35	**608**	197·60	**658**	213·85	**708**	230·10	**758**	246·35	**808**	262·60	**858**	278·85	**908**	295·10	**958**	311·35
509	165·43	**559**	181·68	**609**	197·93	**659**	214·18	**709**	230·43	**759**	246·68	**809**	262·93	**859**	279·18	**909**	295·43	**959**	311·68
510	165·75	**560**	182·00	**610**	198·25	**660**	214·50	**710**	230·75	**760**	247·00	**810**	263·25	**860**	279·50	**910**	295·75	**960**	312·00
511	166·08	**561**	182·33	**611**	198·58	**661**	214·83	**711**	231·08	**761**	247·33	**811**	263·58	**861**	279·83	**911**	296·08	**961**	312·33
512	166·40	**562**	182·65	**612**	198·90	**662**	215·15	**712**	231·40	**762**	247·65	**812**	263·90	**862**	280·15	**912**	296·40	**962**	312·65
513	166·73	**563**	182·98	**613**	199·23	**663**	215·48	**713**	231·73	**763**	247·98	**813**	264·23	**863**	280·48	**913**	296·73	**963**	312·98
514	167·05	**564**	183·30	**614**	199·55	**664**	215·80	**714**	232·05	**764**	248·30	**814**	264·55	**864**	280·80	**914**	297·05	**964**	313·30
515	167·38	**565**	183·63	**615**	199·88	**665**	216·13	**715**	232·38	**765**	248·63	**815**	264·88	**865**	281·13	**915**	297·38	**965**	313·63
516	167·70	**566**	183·95	**616**	200·20	**666**	216·45	**716**	232·70	**766**	248·95	**816**	265·20	**866**	281·45	**916**	297·70	**966**	313·95
517	168·03	**567**	184·28	**617**	200·53	**667**	216·78	**717**	233·03	**767**	249·28	**817**	265·53	**867**	281·78	**917**	298·03	**967**	314·28
518	168·35	**568**	184·60	**618**	200·85	**668**	217·10	**718**	233·35	**768**	249·60	**818**	265·85	**868**	282·10	**918**	298·35	**968**	314·60
519	168·68	**569**	184·93	**619**	201·18	**669**	217·43	**719**	233·68	**769**	249·93	**819**	266·18	**869**	282·43	**919**	298·68	**969**	314·93
520	169·00	**570**	185·25	**620**	201·50	**670**	217·75	**720**	234·00	**770**	250·25	**820**	266·50	**870**	282·75	**920**	299·00	**970**	315·25
521	169·33	**571**	185·58	**621**	201·83	**671**	218·08	**721**	234·33	**771**	250·58	**821**	266·83	**871**	283·08	**921**	299·33	**971**	315·58
522	169·65	**572**	185·90	**622**	202·15	**672**	218·40	**722**	234·65	**772**	250·90	**822**	267·15	**872**	283·40	**922**	299·65	**972**	315·90
523	169·98	**573**	186·23	**623**	202·48	**673**	218·73	**723**	234·98	**773**	251·23	**823**	267·48	**873**	283·73	**923**	299·98	**973**	316·23
524	170·30	**574**	186·55	**624**	202·80	**674**	219·05	**724**	235·30	**774**	251·55	**824**	267·80	**874**	284·05	**924**	300·30	**974**	316·55
525	170·63	**575**	186·88	**625**	203·13	**675**	219·38	**725**	235·63	**775**	251·88	**825**	268·13	**875**	284·38	**925**	300·63	**975**	316·88
526	170·95	**576**	187·20	**626**	203·45	**676**	219·70	**726**	235·95	**776**	252·20	**826**	268·45	**876**	284·70	**926**	300·95	**976**	317·20
527	171·28	**577**	187·53	**627**	203·78	**677**	220·03	**727**	236·28	**777**	252·53	**827**	268·78	**877**	285·03	**927**	301·28	**977**	317·53
528	171·60	**578**	187·85	**628**	204·10	**678**	220·35	**728**	236·60	**778**	252·85	**828**	269·10	**878**	285·35	**928**	301·60	**978**	317·85
529	171·93	**579**	188·18	**629**	204·43	**679**	220·68	**729**	236·93	**779**	253·18	**829**	269·43	**879**	285·68	**929**	301·93	**979**	318·18
530	172·25	**580**	188·50	**630**	204·75	**680**	221·00	**730**	237·25	**780**	253·50	**830**	269·75	**880**	286·00	**930**	302·25	**980**	318·50
531	172·58	**581**	188·83	**631**	205·08	**681**	221·33	**731**	237·58	**781**	253·83	**831**	270·08	**881**	286·33	**931**	302·58	**981**	318·83
532	172·90	**582**	189·15	**632**	205·40	**682**	221·65	**732**	237·90	**782**	254·15	**832**	270·40	**882**	286·65	**932**	302·90	**982**	319·15
533	173·23	**583**	189·48	**633**	205·73	**683**	221·98	**733**	238·23	**783**	254·48	**833**	270·73	**883**	286·98	**933**	303·23	**983**	319·48
534	173·55	**584**	189·80	**634**	206·05	**684**	222·30	**734**	238·55	**784**	254·80	**834**	271·05	**884**	287·30	**934**	303·55	**984**	319·80
535	173·88	**585**	190·13	**635**	206·38	**685**	222·63	**735**	238·88	**785**	255·13	**835**	271·38	**885**	287·63	**935**	303·88	**985**	320·13
536	174·20	**586**	190·45	**636**	206·70	**686**	222·95	**736**	239·20	**786**	255·45	**836**	271·70	**886**	287·95	**936**	304·20	**986**	320·45
537	174·53	**587**	190·78	**637**	207·03	**687**	223·28	**737**	239·53	**787**	255·78	**837**	272·03	**887**	288·28	**937**	304·53	**987**	320·78
538	174·85	**588**	191·10	**638**	207·35	**688**	223·60	**738**	239·85	**788**	256·10	**838**	272·35	**888**	288·60	**938**	304·85	**988**	321·10
539	175·18	**589**	191·43	**639**	207·68	**689**	223·93	**739**	240·18	**789**	256·43	**839**	272·68	**889**	288·93	**939**	305·18	**989**	321·43
540	175·50	**590**	191·75	**640**	208·00	**690**	224·25	**740**	240·50	**790**	256·75	**840**	273·00	**890**	289·25	**940**	305·50	**990**	321·75
541	175·83	**591**	192·08	**641**	208·33	**691**	224·58	**741**	240·83	**791**	257·08	**841**	273·33	**891**	289·58	**941**	305·83	**991**	322·08
542	176·15	**592**	192·40	**642**	208·65	**692**	224·90	**742**	241·15	**792**	257·40	**842**	273·65	**892**	289·90	**942**	306·15	**992**	322·40
543	176·48	**593**	192·73	**643**	208·98	**693**	225·23	**743**	241·48	**793**	257·73	**843**	273·98	**893**	290·23	**943**	306·48	**993**	322·73
544	176·80	**594**	193·05	**644**	209·30	**694**	225·55	**744**	241·80	**794**	258·05	**844**	274·30	**894**	290·55	**944**	306·80	**994**	323·05
545	177·13	**595**	193·38	**645**	209·63	**695**	225·88	**745**	242·13	**795**	258·38	**845**	274·63	**895**	290·88	**945**	307·13	**995**	323·38
546	177·45	**596**	193·70	**646**	209·95	**696**	226·20	**746**	242·45	**796**	258·70	**846**	274·95	**896**	291·20	**946**	307·45	**996**	323·70
547	177·78	**597**	194·03	**647**	210·28	**697**	226·53	**747**	242·78	**797**	259·03	**847**	275·28	**897**	291·53	**947**	307·78	**997**	324·03
548	178·10	**598**	194·35	**648**	210·60	**698**	226·85	**748**	243·10	**798**	259·35	**848**	275·60	**898**	291·85	**948**	308·10	**998**	324·35
549	178·43	**599**	194·68	**649**	210·93	**699**	227·18	**749**	243·43	**799**	259·68	**849**	275·93	**899**	292·18	**949**	308·43	**999**	324·68
550	178·75	**600**	195·00	**650**	211·25	**700**	227·50	**750**	243·75	**800**	260·00	**850**	276·25	**900**	292·50	**950**	308·75	**1000**	325·00

On	**£5,500**	**£6,000**	**£6,500**	**£7,000**	**£7,500**	**£8,000**	**£8,500**	**£9,000**	**£9,500**
Tax	£1,788	£1,950	£2,113	£2,275	£2,438	£2,600	£2,763	£2,925	£3,088

The Budget proposals are introduced by the Chancellor of the Exchequer in the House of Commons.
Note: Please remember that these proposals are subject to amendment during the passage of the Finance Bill through Parliament.

Allowances

	2018/19 (£)	2019/20 (£)
Personal allowance	11,850	12,500
Marriage allowance	1,190	1,250
Married couplles allowance (born before 6 April 1935) – maximum allowance	8,695	8,915
Married couplles allowance - minimum allowance	3,360	3,450
Maximum income before abatement of:		
personal allowance	100,000	100,000
relief for older taxpayers	28,900	29,600
Personal allowance abatement income ceiling	123,700	125,000
Blind person's allowance	2,390	2,450
Dividend allowance	2,000	2,000
Personal savings allowance - basic rate taxpayers	1,000	1,000
Personal savings allowance - higher rate taxpayers	500	500

Income tax rates

Rate on non-dividend savings income	0%	0%
On taxable income up to	2,000*	2,000*

*Starting rate applies to savings income only. If non-savings income is above this limit then the starting rate for savings does not apply.

Basic rate	20%	20%
On taxable income up to	34,500	37,500
Higher rate	40%	40%
On taxable income over	34,500	37,500
Additional rate	45%	45%
On taxable income over	150,000	150,000
Lower rate on dividend income	7.50%	7.50%
Higher rate on dividend income	32.50%	32.50%
Additional higher rate	38.10%	38.10%

Company taxation

	FY2018 and 2019
Corporation tax rates	
Main rate	19%

F(No2)A 2015, s 7(2) sets the main rate of corporation tax for the financial years 2017 to 2019 inclusive at 19%.
FA 2016, s 46 sets the rate at 17% for the financial year 2020.

Inheritance tax

Nil-rate band (frozen for all tax years 2015/16 to 2020/21)	£325,000
Death rate	40%

Additional nil-rate band when residence passed on death to direct descendant:

2017/18	£100,000
2018/19	£125,000
2019/20	£150,000
2020/21	£175,000

Capital gains

	2018/19	2019/20
Rates		
Main rates for individuals	10%/20%*	10%/20%*
Rates for individuals (for gains on residential property not eligible for private residence relief and carried interest)	18%/28%	18%/28%
Main rate for trustees and personal representatives	20%	20%
Rate for trustees and personal representatives (for gains on residential property not eligible for private residence relief)	28%	28%
Entrepreneurs' relief flat rate	10%	10%
General exemption limit	£11,700	£12,000

*Chargeable gains are aggregated with taxable income and to the extent that the aggregate falls above the income tax basic rate threshold, CGT is charged at 20%(taking the chargeable gains as being the highest part of that aggregate). If the aggregate falls below the threshold, the CGT rate will be 10%.

VAT

Standard rate	20%
Registration threshold from 1 April 2019 (remaining unchanged from 1 April 2018)	£85,000

National Insurance

	2019/20 £ per week
Class 1	
Lower earnings limit - primary	118
Upper earnings limit - primary	962
Primary threshold	166
Secondary threshold	166
Upper secondary threshold for under 21s	962
Apprentice upper secondary threshold for under 25s	962
Employee contributution rate between primary and upper earnings limit	12%
Employee contributution rate above upper earnings limit	2%
Employers' secondary rate above secondary threshold	13.80%
Employment Allowance	£3,000
Class 1A and 1B	13.80%
Class 2	
Flat weekly rate	£3.00
Small profits threshold	£6,365
Class 3	
Flat weekly rate	£15.00
Class 4	
Lower profits limit	£8,632
Upper profits limit	£50,000
Rate payable between lower and upper profits limits	9%
Rate payable on profits over upper profits limit	2%

Income tax, capital gains tax, inheritance tax, etc

Income tax

Personal allowance and basic rate limit from 2019/20

For 2019/20, the personal allowance will rise to £12,500 (from £11,850 in 2018/19), and the basic rate limit will be increased to £37,500 (from £34,500 in 2018/19). As a result, the higher rate threshold will be £50,000 in 2019/20.

From 2021/22 onwards, the personal allowance and basic rate limit will be indexed with the consumer price index.

Changes to the basic rate limit and higher rate threshold will apply to non-savings, non-dividend income in England, Wales and Northern Ireland, and to savings and dividend income in the UK.

Van benefit charge and fuel benefit charges for cars and vans from 6 April 2019

From 6 April 2019, the flat-rate van benefit charge will increase to £3,430, the multiplier for the car fuel benefit charge will increase to £24,100, and the flat-rate van fuel benefit charge will increase to £655.

Gift aid small donations scheme

Currently, the gift aid small donations scheme (GASDS) applies to donations of £20 or less made by individuals in cash or by contactless payment. This limit is to be raised to £30. Contactless donations have been included in GASDS from April 2017. The limit for contactless payments in the UK is £30 and raising the small donations limit for GASDS to £30 will be in line with this.

The increase is subject to approval by a resolution of the House of Commons and is expected to take effect from 6 April 2019.

Increases to charities' small trading exemption limits

The small trading tax exemption limits for charities that apply to trading that does not relate to a charity's primary purpose are to be increased from April 2019.

The new limits will be as follows:

- annual charity income under £32,000: maximum non-primary purpose trading is £8,000;
- annual charity income between £32,000 and £320,000: maximum non-primary purpose trading is 25% of income; and
- annual charity income over £320,000: maximum non-primary purpose trading is £80,000.

Income tax, capital gains tax and corporation tax: voluntary tax returns

Historically, HMRC have exercised discretionary collection and management powers to accept and treat voluntary income and corporation tax self-assessment returns received on the same basis as tax returns received under a statutory notice to file.

In the light of recent legal challenges to the practice and the validity of returns received voluntarily, legislation will be introduced with retrospective effect to put the practice onto a statutory basis. This change is intended to remove any doubt for taxpayers that voluntary tax returns have and will continue to be accepted as valid returns. The measure will have retrospective and prospective effect from the date of Royal Assent to Finance Bill 2018–19.

Tax treatment of social security benefits

Legislation is to be introduced to confirm the tax status of four existing and five new social security benefits.

The Scottish Government is introducing five new benefits:

- young carer grant;
- best start grant;

- funeral expense assistance;
- discretionary housing payments; and
- carer's allowance supplement.

Legislation will confirm that the first four are exempt from tax, and that the carer's allowance supplement is taxable.

Legislation will also confirm tax exempt status for the council tax reduction scheme, discretionary housing payments and the flexible support fund overseen by the UK Government and the discretionary support scheme overseen by the Northern Ireland Executive.

The measure will take effect from the date of Royal Assent to the Finance Bill 2018–19.

Capital gains tax

Annual exempt amount

The annual exemption for capital gains tax purposes will increase from £11,700 to £12,000 with effect for gains accruing on and after 6 April 2019.

The annual exemption for trustees of most trusts also rises to £6,000 from the same date.

Entrepreneurs' relief

The qualifying conditions for entrepreneurs' relief (ER) are changing, some with immediate effect.

For a holding of shares or securities to qualify for ER the company must be the taxpayer's personal company, which until now has meant holding at least 5% of the ordinary share capital and 5% of the associated voting rights. This condition is tweaked so that the individual must also hold 5% of the economic rights in the company, ie a right to 5% of the net assets of the company and to 5% of the distributable profits. This additional condition applies for all disposals made on and after 29 October 2018.

Currently, all the conditions for ER must be met for at least one year to the date of sale, or if the business has ceased, to the last day of trading. From 6 April 2019, all of the qualifying conditions, including the new economic rights condition described above, must be met for at least two years ending with the date of disposal or of cessation of trading. However, if the business ceased trading before 29 October 2018, the one-year qualifying period will still apply to the gains arising from the disposal of shares or assets disposed of after cessation.

Main residence relief

There are two changes to restrict the scope of the CGT relief for gains arising from disposal of the taxpayer's main residence. Both of these changes are due to come into effect from 6 April 2020 after a period of consultation.

Where the property has been let at any time, each owner can claim lettings relief to cover gains of up to £40,000. This relief is capped at the amount of CGT relief due in respect of the period in which the owner was actually occupying the property. The government is proposing to restrict lettings relief to only cover periods during which the owner is occupying the same property as the tenant.

Currently, the CGT relief for a main residence covers the last 18 months of ownership, even if the owner is not in occupation during that final period. The government is proposing to cut this CGT exemption for the final ownership period, when the owner is not in occupation, to nine months. However, a 36-month final period of CGT exemption will continue to apply for disabled owners or those who have moved to live in residential care.

Gains by non-UK residents

Individuals who are not resident in the UK must pay CGT on gains arising on UK residential property, for periods from 6 April 2015. The tax arising from the sale has to be paid within 30 days of the completion of the sale, unless the taxpayer is within self-assessment. This exception to paying the CGT due within 30 days is removed from 6 April 2019.

The liability to tax on gains will be extended to disposals of non-residential property with effect from 1 April 2019 (for companies) or 6 April 2019 (for individuals and trusts). Only the gain accruing after that date will be charged to tax.

Payment by UK residents

UK resident individuals and trusts who make gains from UK residential property will need to make a payment on account of CGT within 30 days of the completion date, for disposals completed on or after 6 April 2020.

This new reporting and payment deadline will not apply where the gain is fully exempt from CGT.

Inheritance tax

Changes to residence nil rate band

Minor technical amendments are to be made to the residence nil rate band (RNRB) for inheritance tax (IHT) purposes. The amendments seek to clarify the working of the downsizing rules and provide certainty over when a person is treated as 'inheriting' property.

Finance Bill 2018–19 will include provisions to ensure that the value of any part of a residence that is inherited by an exempt beneficiary is taken into account in determining a person's lost relievable amount. New provisions will also ensure that where a residence forms part of a person's estate immediately before their death as a gift with reservation of benefit (in accordance with FA 1986, s 102(3)), it will only be treated as being inherited by a direct descendant if the property became immediately comprised in the direct descendant's estate as a result of the original gift. These changes will have effect for deaths applying on or after 29 October 2018.

National Insurance and pensions

National insurance

National Insurance rates and threshold

The National Insurance rates and threshold applying for 2019/20 have been announced.

For Class 1 purposes, the lower earnings limit is set at £118 per week, the primary and secondary threshold at £166 per week and the upper earnings limit at £962 per week. The upper secondary threshold for under 21s and the apprentice secondary threshold are also set at £962 per week. The main and primary rates of Class 1 contributions remain unchanged at, respectively, 12% and 2%, while the secondary rate and Class 1A and 1B rates remain at 13.8%.

The self-employed will continue to pay both Class 2 and Class 4 contributions in 2019/20. Class 2 contributions, payable where profits exceed the small profits threshold, set at £6,365 for 2019/20 rises to £3 per week. Self-employed earners with profits below the small profits threshold can pay Class 2 contributions voluntarily. The lower profits limit for Class 4 contributions is increased to £8,632 for 2019/20, and the upper profits limit is increased to £50,000. The main rate remains at 9% and the additional rate at 2%.

The rate of voluntary Class 3 contributions rises to £15 per week for 2019/20.

National Insurance Contributions Bill

As announced on 6 September 2018, the planned abolition of Class 2 National Insurance contributions and reform of Class 4 contributions, which were due to take effect from 6 April 2019, will now not go ahead.

However, the government is to legislate for the two remaining measures included in the draft National Insurance Contributions Bill: the introduction of a Class 1A (employer-only) charge on termination payments in excess of £30,000 and sporting testimonials in excess of £100,000. Both measures will take effect from 6

April 2020, rather than from 6 April 2019 as previously intended.

Employment allowance restriction

The National Insurance employment allowance, which provides employers with a reduction of up to £3,000 in their employer's Class 1 National Insurance contributions bill, is to be restricted from 6 April 2020, so that it will only be available to employers whose National Insurance bill was less than £100,000 in the previous tax year.

The measure will target the employment allowance to support smaller businesses.

Pensions

Lifetime allowance

The lifetime allowance for pension savings is increased to £1,055,000 for 2019/20.

Corporation tax, business tax, etc

Corporation tax

Non-UK resident companies owning UK land to be subject to corporation tax on income and gains

There are two measures which affect non-resident companies investing in UK property:

- From April 2020, non-resident companies will pay corporation tax on their income profits instead of being charged under the income tax rules.
- From April 2019, all non-resident property investors will be taxed on property gains, irrespective of whether the property is held for residential or commercial purposes. Furthermore, the tax will apply to property held indirectly through another vehicle such as a company or partnership.

Corporation tax on income profits

This charge will replace the income tax charge which normally applies to non-UK resident corporate investors. The effect of bringing offshore companies into the corporation tax net is to ensure that they are subject to the same restrictions on interest relief and losses that apply to UK companies.

Various supplementary and transitional rules will apply:

- There will be rules to ensure that no double counting of income or expenses occurs as a result of the transition. For example, it is in theory possible for an amount to be taxed or relieved both under the income tax rules and under the corporation tax rules during the transition period.
- The transition will not give rise to a disposal event for capital allowances purposes, thereby avoiding any balancing charges or allowances from arising.
- The company will not be required to notify HMRC that it is now subject to corporation tax in cases where its only UK income source is its UK property business and where any UK tax deducted from its rental income fully satisfies its corporation tax liability.
- The company will be able to carry forward losses which would previously have been allowable as income tax losses in order for offset against its corporation tax profits in respect of its UK property business profits.
- Deductions from derivative contracts referable to the pre-commencement period will be permitted, but only if the amount would have been deductible under the income tax rules. So no deduction is allowable for capital amounts, even though this is normally permitted for corporation tax purposes.

- Hedging derivatives will in general, continue to benefit from the Disregard Regulations (SI 2004/3256).

The operative date for the changes is 6 April 2020.

Corporation tax on chargeable gains

At present, non-resident companies are subject to chargeable gains on the following:

- a charge on the disposal of residential property subject to capital gains tax (the 'NRCGT' charge) – this applies only to closely held non-resident companies; and
- a charge on the disposal of residential property which is subject to the annual tax on enveloped dwellings (ATED) regime ('ATED-related CGT').

From 6 April 2019, these charges will be replaced by a single charge to corporation tax on chargeable gains. Various rebasing will ensure that only post-April 2019 gains and losses are captured. However, the company will have the option to bring the entire gain or loss within the tax charge. An election is likely to be made where there is a post-April 2019 gain, but the taxpayer has suffered an overall loss on its investment.

In addition to the tax on directly held property, non-residents will also be taxed on gains where property is held indirectly through an intermediate vehicle such as a company or partnership or other entity. This ensures that property gains can still be taxed where the non-resident company disposes of its interest in the relevant entity by selling its shares or partnership interest.

Changes to the definition of permanent establishment

This is a measure that is designed to prevent overseas companies from artificially fragmenting their activities in order to avoid having a permanent establishment in the UK.

Under the current rules, a non-resident company has a taxable presence if it trades in the UK through a permanent establishment (CTA 2009, s 5). A company has a permanent establishment in the UK if either (see CTA 2010, s 1141(1)):

- it has a fixed place of business there through which the business of the company is wholly or partly carried on; or
- an agent acting on behalf of the company has and habitually exercises their authority to do business on behalf of the company.

Certain preparatory or auxiliary activities in the UK fall outside the scope of the definition. These include activities such as storing the company's own products, purchasing goods, or collecting information (CTA 2010, s 1143). Under the new proposals, this exemption will be denied in cases where these activities form part of a fragmented business operation. In particular, a non-resident company will have a UK permanent establishment if:

- the company, either alone or with related entities (whether foreign or UK), carries on a cohesive business operation, either at the same place, or at different places in the UK;
- at least one of them has a permanent establishment where complementary functions are carried on; and
- all the activities together would create a permanent establishment if they were in a single company.

The operative date is accounting periods beginning on or after 1 January 2019. Accounting periods which straddle this date are treated as two separate accounting periods, one ending on 31 December 2018 and the other starting on 1 January 2019.

Offshore receipts from intangible property

New rules will apply an income tax charge to overseas entities in a low tax jurisdiction who receive intangible property receipts which are referable to the sale of goods or services in the UK. For example:

- a UK entity receives income from selling goods or services in the UK;
- the UK seller then makes a royalty payment to an offshore entity for which it can claim a tax deduction in the UK;
- the offshore entity is subject to minimal tax rates on the royalty payment.

The new rules will include the following:

- a UK income tax charge on the owners of intangible property or those that are entitled to income that is referable to the sale of goods or services in the UK in relation to that intangible property and who are not resident in a full treaty territory;
- provisions to ensure joint and several liability for the tax where persons who are within the same control group may also be liable in the event that the owner or other person entitled to the offshore receipt fails to pay; and
- anti-avoidance and anti-forestalling rules will be in place to counter any arrangements designed to avoid the new tax charge. These rules affect arrangements entered into on or after 29 October 2018, where one of the main purposes of the arrangement is to either avoid the charge, or to mitigate or reduce the charge under a double tax treaty.

There will also be a number of exemptions:

- The rules do not affect partnerships which are regarded as separate entities for tax purposes and are resident in full treaty territories.
- The rules will not apply where the value of UK sales is less than £10 million in a given tax year.
- The rules will not apply where all, or substantially all, of the business activity in relation to the intangible property has always taken place in the territory of residence.
- The rules will not apply where the tax paid in relation to the relevant income is at least 50% of the UK income tax that would otherwise arise under this measure.

The operative date for the provisions is generally 6 April 2019, but with targeted anti-avoidance rules to apply to forestalling arrangements entered into on or after 29 October 2018.

New statutory remedy in relation to advance corporation tax

This measure applies to companies that have made common law claims against HMRC in relation to the operation of the former advance corporation tax (ACT) regime. It provides a non-exclusive interest return in respect of ACT which was paid and subsequently set-off or repaid.

Legislation will be introduced in Finance Bill 2018–19 to introduce the new non-exclusive statutory remedy, which effectively provides an interest return on ACT that was paid and set-off or repaid, together with interest on that sum. The measure will have effect on and after the date of Royal Assent to the Finance Bill.

Hybrid instruments

There are a number of measures which are designed to prevent tax mismatches in hybrid instruments. A hybrid is an instrument issued by a company and has features which relate to two or more different classes of security. For example, a company may issue loan capital which gives the holder the right to convert the loan into shares.

Mismatches in tax treatment can arise where the parties to the instrument are resident in different jurisdictions.

The measures include the following:

- changes to the UK's hybrid and other mismatch legislation which are designed to align the UK tax treatment with the latest version of EU Directive 2016/1164 (Anti-Tax Avoidance Directive); and
- a reform to the way that hybrid loans are taxed (hybrid capital instruments).

Amendment of hybrid and mismatch rules to align with EU Directive

There are two measures:

- The first measure relates to the treatment of certain mismatches involving permanent establishments. This is targeted at cases where a company has a permanent establishment which is recognised by the jurisdiction where it is resident, but not by the jurisdiction where the permanent establishment itself is located. A permanent establishment which is disregarded in the place where it is located will now fall within the scope of the mismatch rules.
- The second measure relates to the treatment of certain types of regulatory capital which are exempt under the mismatch rules. Regulations will be enacted to provide a revised definition of exempt regulatory capital to align the UK tax treatment with the requirements of EU Directive 2016/1164.

The change in relation to disregarded permanent establishments included in this measure have effect from 1 January 2020. The regulatory power in relation to the treatment of regulatory capital included in this measure will have effect from 1 January 2019.

Taxation of hybrid capital instruments

The new rules on hybrid capital instruments are targeted at loan capital which has equity features and which allows for the deferral or cancellation of interest payments. If these instruments meet certain specified conditions:

- any interest payable will be deductible for the issuer and taxable for the holder; and
- a transfer of the instrument will be exempt from both stamp duty and stamp duty reserve tax.

In addition, measures will be introduced to ensure that when a company issues loan capital and the funds are passed internally within the company's group, both internal and external loan relationships are taxed on the same basis.

The operative date is accounting periods beginning on or after 1 January 2019. Accounting periods which straddle this date are treated as two separate accounting periods, one ending on 31 December 2018 and the other starting on 1 January 2019.

Diverted profits tax

The diverted profits tax (DPT) rules are targeted at multinational groups whereby arrangements are made to artificially shift profits away from the UK to low tax jurisdictions. The rules are to be amended in order to close a tax planning opportunity, as well as clarifying that the tax only applies once. There are also a number of minor amendments.

In particular:

- The new measures will close a tax planning opportunity, whereby a company can amend its corporation tax return after the review period has ended and the various DPT time limits have expired. A review period is (currently) a 12-month period following a DPT payment by the company which allows HMRC to determine whether any adjustments need to be made to the charge.
- Diverted profits will only be taxed once, either as a payment under the DPT rules or under the standard corporation tax rules, but not both.
- The review period is to be extended from 12 months to 15 months. The company's right to amend its corporation tax return during the review period will also be extended but only for the purpose of including the diverted profits into its corporation tax calculation.
- Amendments will also make clear that diverted profits liable to DPT can be reduced by amendment to the company's corporation tax return during the first 12 months of the review period.

The operative date for the above is 29 October 2018.

Capital allowances

Clarification of allowances for costs of altering land

Legislation is to be introduced in the Finance Bill 2018–19 with effect for claims made on or after 29 October 2018 to clarify the scope of relief given by CAA 2001, ss 21–22 for expenditure incurred in altering land. The changes will make it clear that the allowances are only available for expenditure altering land for the installation of qualifying plant and machinery, which itself qualifies for capital allowances, and not for expenditure incurred altering land for the installation of assets which do not qualify for capital allowances.

Capital allowances for structures and buildings

A new capital allowance for structures and buildings is introduced from 29 October 2018. The new structures and buildings allowance will be available for eligible construction costs on new non-residential structures incurred on or after 29 October 2018. The allowance will be given at an annual rate of 2% on a straight-line basis.

The aim of the relief is to relieve the costs of physically constructing new structures and buildings that are intended for commercial use. The relief will be available both to businesses chargeable to income tax and to those chargeable to corporation tax.

A technical note explaining the new relief is available on the gov.uk website: www.gov.uk/government/publications/capital-allowances-for-structures-and-buildings-technical-note.

Ending enhanced capital allowances for energy and water efficient plant and machinery

Legislation is to be introduced in the Finance Bill 2018–19 to remove the first-year allowances scheme for products on the energy technology list and the water technology list, including the associated tax credit, with effect from 1 April 2020 for companies and 6 April 2020 for unincorporated businesses.

First-year allowance for electric charge points

The current 100% first-year allowance for expenditure on electric charge point equipment is to be extended by four years. As a result, the allowance will now come to an end on 31 March 2023 for corporation tax purposes and on 5 April 2023 for income tax purposes.

Reduction of rate of special writing down allowance

The rate of writing down allowance for the plant and machinery special rate pool is reduced from 8% to 6% with effect from 1 April 2019 for corporation tax purposes and from 6 April 2019 for income tax purposes. Where the chargeable period spans 1 April/6 April (as appropriate), a hybrid rate will apply to unrelieved expenditure in the special rate pool based on the proportion of the chargeable period falling before the change date and the corresponding proportion falling after the change date.

Special rate expenditure includes expenditure on long-life assets, thermal insulation, integral features and expenditure on high emission cars (110g/km where the expenditure is incurred on or after 1 April 2018).

Temporary increase in the annual investment allowance

The annual investment allowance (AIA) is to be increased from £200,000 to £1 million for the two-year period from 1 January 2019 to 31 December 2020. It will revert to the permanent level of £200,000 from 1 January 2021.

Where a business has a chargeable period that spans either 1 January 2019 or 1 January 2021, transitional rules will apply under which the AIA will be computed in two parts. Where the period spans 1 January 2019, the allowance will be calculated by reference to an AIA of £200,000 for the period before 1 January 2019 and by reference to an AIA of £1 million for the period after the change. The reverse will apply where the period spans 1 January 2021.

VAT, customs duties, etc

VAT

Changes to the VAT specified supplies anti-avoidance

This measure amends the Value Added Tax (Input Tax) (Specified Supplies) Order 1999, art 3 to restrict its application in certain circumstances in order to prevent avoidance.

The Specified Supplies Order allows companies who export certain financial services from the European Union (EU) to reclaim the VAT they incur while providing those services. When these services are supplied inside the EU, this VAT cannot be reclaimed.

The Specified Supplies Order is currently being exploited by companies that form arrangements with organisations outside of the EU to re-supply or 'loop' those services back to UK consumers, allowing themselves to reclaim the VAT and thereby gaining a competitive advantage over purely UK based companies.

This order seeks to prevent a particular form of this 'looping' involving insurance intermediaries by restricting the application of the specified supplies order to cases where the final consumer is not in the UK, as was intended.

Changes to the VAT treatment of vouchers

This measure introduces legislation providing for the VAT treatment of vouchers issued on or after 1 January 2019. It affects only vouchers for which a payment has been made and which will be used to buy something. The measure does not apply to vouchers issued before 1 January 2019, for which existing rules will continue to apply.

Vouchers, in this context, are gift cards and gift tokens, with examples including simple book tokens, gift vouchers, and electronic vouchers purchased from specialist businesses. The changes do not apply to discount vouchers or money-off tokens.

Under current UK VAT legislation, the customer is deemed to be receiving two supplies: (1) a voucher; and (2) an underlying supply of goods or services. The measure makes it clear that for VAT purposes there will no longer be a separate supply of a voucher. Instead, the rules will be simplified so that there is only the supply of the underlying goods or services, which will be provided in exchange for the voucher at a later date.

Reverse charge anti-avoidance changes

This measure does not directly affect any businesses or customers but provides a power to make regulations to amend certain anti-avoidance provisions.

The anti-avoidance provisions were introduced to discourage attempts by fraudsters to escape a reverse charge measure by making supplies to non-VAT registered businesses instead and charging VAT.

This measure will allow regulations to be made to prevent unintended consequences for small businesses trading below the VAT threshold. It will provide the government with the power to relieve burdens on small businesses by removing the requirement to include the value of reverse charge supplies received in the value of their taxable turnover.

Where that option is exercised, it will ensure that small businesses receiving supplies within the scope of the specified reverse charge are not forced into registering for VAT where they would otherwise not be required to.

Registration thresholds

The VAT registration threshold will remain unchanged for another two years from 1 April 2020 to 31 March 2022.

Customs duties, etc

Alcohol duty: increase in rates

The following duty rates will be frozen:

- duty rates on beer;
- duty rates on spirits and other drinks above 22% alcohol by volume (abv);
- duty rates on still cider and perry, and lower-strength sparkling cider and perry;

The duty rates on wine and made-wine at or below 22% abv, and high-strength sparkling cider above 5.5% abv will rise by retail price index inflation from 1 February 2019.

Landfill tax: increase in rates

Landfill tax rates will increase from 1 April 2019. The standard rate will be £91.35 per tonne and the lower rate will be £2.90 per tonne.

Air passenger duty: rates from 1 April 2020 to 31 March 2021

The long-haul rates of air passenger duty (APD) for the tax year 2020 to 2021 will increase in line with the retail price index as forecast at Autumn Budget 2018. Short haul rates will not rise. The reduced rate will therefore be £80, the standard rate will be £176 and the higher rate £528.

Carbon emissions tax

This measure will take effect only if the UK leaves the EU without an agreement. In a 'no deal' scenario, the UK would cease to participate in the EU emissions trading system (ETS) from exit day. This measure would introduce a tax on carbon dioxide emissions (and other greenhouse gas emissions on a carbon equivalent basis) produced by UK stationary installations currently in the EU ETS.

The new tax will be introduced from 1 April 2019, with the first tax period ending on 31 December 2019. The tax would be known as carbon emissions tax, and would be collected by HMRC annually, with the first payment due in 2020.

All current participants in the EU ETS who are UK permit holders operating stationary installations currently in the EU ETS would be set an annual emissions allowance for the purposes of the tax.

For permit holders outside the simplified reporting scheme, this would be based on the allocation of free EU allowances that would have been allocated to installations under Phase 3 of the EU ETS.

Installations would continue to report their activities annually under the existing monitoring, reporting and verification (MRV) scheme and, as at present, this information would establish how many tonnes of greenhouse gases they emit during the reporting period. All emissions that exceed the annual allowance would be taxed on a carbon equivalent basis at a rate for 2019 of £16 per tonne.

Movement of soft drinks between the Isle of Man and UK under soft drinks industry levy

This measure will mean that the movement of liable soft drinks between the UK and Isle of Man will not be seen as either an import or an export under the levy, as long as the levy rates of the UK and Isle of Man remain aligned. It also adds the levy to the list of common duties of the UK and Isle of Man.

Penalty for late submission or failure to submit a return soft drinks industry levy

This measure allows penalties to be raised where those registered for the soft drinks industry levy (SDIL) do not submit their quarterly returns in a timely manner. Legislation will also be amended to allow a penalty to be raised for non-payment of SDIL.

Remote gaming duty: increase in rate

The rate of remote gaming duty will be increased to 21% from 1 October 2019.

Tobacco products duty rates

The duty rate on all tobacco products will continue to increase by 2% above retail price index (RPI) inflation. It was also announced that hand-rolling tobacco will rise by an additional 1%, to 3% above RPI inflation this year.

The new tobacco duty rates have effect from 6pm on 29 October 2018 with the exception of tobacco for heating, which will take effect on 1 July 2019 after relevant amendments are made to secondary legislation.

Stamp Taxes

Stamp duty land tax

Higher rates of stamp duty land tax for additional dwellings – minor amendments

There are a number of changes to the rules relating to the higher rates of stamp duty land tax (SDLT) for additional dwellings. Currently, purchasers of residential dwellings pay an additional 3% SDLT when certain conditions apply – principally if, when the new dwelling is acquired, they already owned an interest in another dwelling. This additional rate is often referred to as HRAD.

HRAD does not apply to a purchaser replacing their main residential dwelling. In order not to prevent acquisitions of new dwellings where the old home cannot be sold or where a sale is delayed, relief from HRAD is extended to enable purchasers who buy a new home before their current home is sold to retrospectively claim relief once their current dwelling is sold, provided that it is sold within three years.

There are time limits on when this relief from HRAD must be claimed in these circumstances, which will now be extended for purchases where the old main residence was sold on or after 29 October 2018. Claims can now be made within 12 months of the later either of the sale of the previous main residence or the filing date of the SDLT return for the new residence on which HRAD was paid.

HRAD applies to an acquisition of a 'major interest' in land and there is now a clarification that this includes 'undivided share' in land, confirming HMRC's current practice.

First-time buyers' relief and shared ownership

Purchasers of certain shared ownership dwellings (eg from a local housing authority or housing association) may be eligible for relief from SDLT. The purchaser of a qualifying dwelling can choose whether SDLT applies on the initial purchase based on the then market value or on the initial payment and then each time an additional interest in the property is acquired (once 80% has been acquired).

Relief for first-time buyers currently applies where SDLT is paid on the market value and will be extended to include purchases of qualifying shared ownership property where the purchaser chooses not to make a market value election but to pay SDLT in stages.

Where the market value of the shared ownership property is £500,000 or less, the SDLT rates for first-time buyers will be applied to the first share purchased. Relief will also apply to the rental payments.

The changes will take effect on 29 October 2018 and will apply retrospectively from 22 November 2017. Purchasers can claim a refund of tax if the effective date of their purchase was on or after 22 November 2017, provided the purchase would now qualify for first-time buyers' relief. Refunds for SDLT paid on the rent can also be claimed by purchasers who have made a market value election.

Consultation on SDLT additional charge for non-residents

The government will publish a consultation in January 2019 on a proposed SDLT surcharge of 1% for non-residents buying residential property in England and Northern Ireland.

Changes to the filing and payment process

As has been discussed for some time and was confirmed at Autumn Budget 2017, the time limit to file a SDLT return and pay the tax due will reduce from 30 days to 14 days for transactions with an effective date on or after 1 March 2019. Interest on late payments will start from the new 14-day deadline.

The forms used for SDLT land transaction returns will also be amended on or before 1 March 2019.

Stamp duty, etc

Stamp duty, stamp duty reserve tax and stamp duty land tax – exemption for financial institutions in resolution

Legislation will be introduced in Finance Bill 2018–19 to ensure that stamp duty, stamp duty reserve tax (SDRT) and stamp duty land tax (SDLT) are not chargeable on the exercise of resolution powers under the UK special resolution regime for managing failed financial institutions.

The exemption will be limited to certain transfers of securities issued by, and to securities and land held by, a failed institution in resolution, to a temporary holding entity appointed by the Bank of England or to a temporary public body and affected creditors. It will not apply:

- to an instrument or order transferring the failed institution's issued share capital or a transfer of its assets to a third-party purchaser following exercise of a private sector purchaser resolution stabilisation power; or
- where, under the terms of the resolution, the institution's issued share capital and/or its assets are onward transferred from a temporary resolution holding entity or public body to a third-party purchaser

These transfers will be subject to a charge to stamp duty, SDRT or SDLT in the usual way. The measure will have effect on and after the date of Royal Assent to Finance Bill 2018–19.

Stamp duty, stamp duty reserve tax and stamp duty land tax – shares consideration rules

Stamp duty and SDRT on shares and securities have separate 'market value consideration' rules for transfers between connected persons. This creates complexity and may lead to avoidance. The government will launch a consultation on 7 November 2018 to consider a single rule to cover both regimes for the transfer of shares (possibly extending to securities).

Legislation will be introduced in Finance Bill 2018–19 to provide for a new market value rule for stamp duty and SDRT for all cases where listed securities are transferred to a company (whether or not for consideration), and the person transferring the securities is connected with the company.

In order to prevent forestalling and avoidance, the government published draft legislation in the Budget introducing a targeted 'market value' rule, applying if listed securities are transferred by a person (or its nominee) to a connected company (or its nominee) and stamp taxes group relief is not available. This rule has immediate effect from 29 October 2018.

'Listed securities' are stock or marketable securities regularly traded on a regulated market, a multilateral trading facility or a recognised foreign exchange. 'Connection' has the meaning set out in CTA 2010, s 1122 and is broadly a question of control.

For stamp duty purposes:

- If the transfer is for consideration consisting of money, stock or security, or the release, assumption or satisfaction of debt, the consideration is deemed, for these purposes, to be the higher of that consideration and the value of the transferred securities (being the price that they might reasonably be expected to fetch on a sale in the open market at that time).

- In other cases (that is, transfers for other non-monetary consideration or no consideration), the consideration is deemed to be the value of the listed securities.

For SDRT purposes, if the agreement is to transfer securities for consideration in money or money's worth, the consideration is deemed, for these purposes, to be the higher of that consideration and the value of the transferred securities.

In other cases, the consideration is deemed to be the value of the listed securities.

If there is an arrangement to transfer the securities to a depositary receipt issuer or into a clearance service and the consideration for the transfer is less than the value of the securities at that time, the consideration is deemed to be that value.

Stamp duty and stamp duty reserve tax – taxation of regulatory capital securities regulations and taxation of hybrid capital instruments

Some companies raise funds by issuing hybrid capital instruments (HCI) which sit close to the border between debt and equity. This is common in the financial sector, where banks and insurers have requirements as to the amount of capital. This means determining the correct tax treatment can be problematic, leading to uncertainty for companies. In conjunction with a review of the corporation tax treatment (to allow deduction of payments under HCI for corporation tax purposes) the government has introduced taxation of hybrid capital instruments (which can be issued by any sector).

There is currently an exemption for stamp duty and SDRT purposes, which will be replaced with a new exemption to take effect for transfers of relevant instruments on or after 29 October 2018.

Stamp duty and stamp duty reserve tax – share incentive plans legislation

Legislation will be introduced in Finance Bill 2018–19 with retrospective effect, to amend the reference in FA 2001, s 95 concerning stamp duty and SDRT relief for share incentive plans (SIPs).

Currently, this refers to 'approved share incentive plans' or 'approved SIPs' whereas other legislation refers to SIPs as 'Schedule 2 SIPs'. This was the result of an oversight and these will be changed to 'Schedule 2 SIPS'. This will not impact on the basis on which the relief is available.

Annual tax on enveloped dwellings

Annual chargeable amounts for the 2019 to 2020 chargeable period

The annual tax on enveloped dwellings (ATED) charges will rise in line with inflation for the 2019/20 chargeable period, beginning 1 April 2019. The charges for 2019/20 are based on the September 2018 consumer price index, which was a 2.4% increase, and rounded down to the nearest £50.

The new ATED charges for the 2019/20 chargeable period are as follows:

Taxable value of the property	*Current charges for the 2018/19 period*	*Increased charges for the 2019/20 chargeable period (From 1 April 2019)*
£500,001 to £1,000,000	£3,600	£3,650
£1,000,001 to £2,000,000	£7,250	£7,400
£2,000,001 to £5,000,000	£24,250	£24,800

Taxable value of the property	*Current charges for the 2018/19 period*	*Increased charges for the 2019/20 chargeable period (From 1 April 2019)*
£5,000,001 to £10,000,000	£56,550	£57,900
£10,000,001 to £20,000,000	£113,400	£116,100
£20,000,001 and over	£226,950	£232,350

Tax administration, anti-avoidance, etc

Tax administration

Amendments to tax legislation to reflect EU exit

This measure allows minor and consequential amendments to be made to tax law to enable it to continue to work in the same way as it does now if the UK leaves the EU without a deal.

The measure provides for three changes:

1. It allows the government to make minor amendments for the purposes of maintaining the effect of the tax legislation, for example, replacing reference to 'EU' with references to 'EU and UK'.
2. It amends an existing power which permits the government to bring international tax agreements into effect in UK law.
3. It introduces a measure which removes reference to EU legislation when HMRC are considering whether, and to what extent, a taxpayer is unjustly enriched by repayment of insurance premium tax, landfill tax or excise duty.

Changes to interest provision for late payment, repayment and penalties

The detail of how interest is applied to late payments for corporation tax, stamp duty and stamp duty land tax and to penalties for failure to comply with obligations is to be clarified.

The measure will also clarify and confirm the basis for interest calculation in respect of the diverted profits tax and repayment supplement by HMRC and will ensure that the interest provisions in Finance Act 2009 apply in relation to penalties charged under the promoters of tax avoidance schemes legislation.

National Insurance Contributions – From 6 April 2019

CLASS 1: EMPLOYED PERSONS	
Rates for **Employees:**	
(a) Employees under state pension age	
Earnings up to £166 p.w.	Nil
Earnings between £166 and £962 p.w.	12.0%
Earnings over £962 p.w.	2.0%
(b) Employees over state pension age	Nil
(c) Married women and widows liable at reduced rate	
Earnings up to £166 p.w.	Nil
Earnings between £166 p.w. and £962 p.w	5.85%
Earnings over £962 p.w.	2.0%
Rates for **Employers:**	
Employees aged under 21/Apprentices aged under 25:	
Earnings up to £962 pw	0%
Earnings over £962 pw	13.8%
Employees aged over 21:	
Earnings up to £962 p.w.	Nil
Earnings over £962 p.w.	13.8%
EMPLOYMENT ALLOWANCE	£3,000 per year, per employer
CLASS 2: SELF-EMPLOYED PERSONS	
Exemption claimable if anticipated earnings less than £6,365	£3.00 p.w.
CLASS 3: VOLUNTARY CONTRIBUTIONS	£15.00 p.w.
CLASS 4: SELF-EMPLOYED PERSONS	
Rate payable on profits between £8,632 and £50,000 per year	9.0%
Over £50,000 per year	2.0%
National Living Wage/National Minimum Wage rates from 1 April 2019:	
	Minimum hourly rate
– aged 25 and over	£8.21
– aged 21 to 24	£7.70
– aged 18 to 20	£6.15
– under 18	£4.35
– Apprentice rate	£3.90

Apprentices are entitled to the apprentice rate if they're either:

- aged under 19; or
- aged 19 or over and in the first year of their apprenticeship

2018/19 and 2019/20: Dividend Trust Rate 37·5%

£ or p	Tax £ or p	£ or p	Tax £ or p	£	Tax £	£	Tax £	£	Tax £	£	Tax £	£	Tax £	£	Tax £	£	Tax £	£	Tax £
1	0·38	**51**	19·13	**101**	37·88	**151**	56·63	**201**	75·38	**251**	94·13	**301**	112·88	**351**	131·63	**401**	150·38	**451**	169·13
2	0·75	**52**	19·50	**102**	38·25	**152**	57·00	**202**	75·75	**252**	94·50	**302**	113·25	**352**	132·00	**402**	150·75	**452**	169·50
3	1·13	**53**	19·88	**103**	38·63	**153**	57·38	**203**	76·13	**253**	94·88	**303**	113·63	**353**	132·38	**403**	151·13	**453**	169·88
4	1·50	**54**	20·25	**104**	39·00	**154**	57·75	**204**	76·50	**254**	95·25	**304**	114·00	**354**	132·75	**404**	151·50	**454**	170·25
5	1·88	**55**	20·63	**105**	39·38	**155**	58·13	**205**	76·88	**255**	95·63	**305**	114·38	**355**	133·13	**405**	151·88	**455**	170·63
6	2·25	**56**	21·00	**106**	39·75	**156**	58·50	**206**	77·25	**256**	96·00	**306**	114·75	**356**	133·50	**406**	152·25	**456**	171·00
7	2·63	**57**	21·38	**107**	40·13	**157**	58·88	**207**	77·63	**257**	96·38	**307**	115·13	**357**	133·88	**407**	152·63	**457**	171·38
8	3·00	**58**	21·75	**108**	40·50	**158**	59·25	**208**	78·00	**258**	96·75	**308**	115·50	**358**	134·25	**408**	153·00	**458**	171·75
9	3·38	**59**	22·13	**109**	40·88	**159**	59·63	**209**	78·38	**259**	97·13	**309**	115·88	**359**	134·63	**409**	153·38	**459**	172·13
10	3·75	**60**	22·50	**110**	41·25	**160**	60·00	**210**	78·75	**260**	97·50	**310**	116·25	**360**	135·00	**410**	153·75	**460**	172·50
11	4·13	**61**	22·88	**111**	41·63	**161**	60·38	**211**	79·13	**261**	97·88	**311**	116·63	**361**	135·38	**411**	154·13	**461**	172·88
12	4·50	**62**	23·25	**112**	42·00	**162**	60·75	**212**	79·50	**262**	98·25	**312**	117·00	**362**	135·75	**412**	154·50	**462**	173·25
13	4·88	**63**	23·63	**113**	42·38	**163**	61·13	**213**	79·88	**263**	98·63	**313**	117·38	**363**	136·13	**413**	154·88	**463**	173·63
14	5·25	**64**	24·00	**114**	42·75	**164**	61·50	**214**	80·25	**264**	99·00	**314**	117·75	**364**	136·50	**414**	155·25	**464**	174·00
15	5·63	**65**	24·38	**115**	43·13	**165**	61·88	**215**	80·63	**265**	99·38	**315**	118·13	**365**	136·88	**415**	155·63	**465**	174·38
16	6·00	**66**	24·75	**116**	43·50	**166**	62·25	**216**	81·00	**266**	99·75	**316**	118·50	**366**	137·25	**416**	156·00	**466**	174·75
17	6·38	**67**	25·13	**117**	43·88	**167**	62·63	**217**	81·38	**267**	100·13	**317**	118·88	**367**	137·63	**417**	156·38	**467**	175·13
18	6·75	**68**	25·50	**118**	44·25	**168**	63·00	**218**	81·75	**268**	100·50	**318**	119·25	**368**	138·00	**418**	156·75	**468**	175·50
19	7·13	**69**	25·88	**119**	44·63	**169**	63·38	**219**	82·13	**269**	100·88	**319**	119·63	**369**	138·38	**419**	157·13	**469**	175·88
20	7·50	**70**	26·25	**120**	45·00	**170**	63·75	**220**	82·50	**270**	101·25	**320**	120·00	**370**	138·75	**420**	157·50	**470**	176·25
21	7·88	**71**	26·63	**121**	45·38	**171**	64·13	**221**	82·88	**271**	101·63	**321**	120·38	**371**	139·13	**421**	157·88	**471**	176·63
22	8·25	**72**	27·00	**122**	45·75	**172**	64·50	**222**	83·25	**272**	102·00	**322**	120·75	**372**	139·50	**422**	158·25	**472**	177·00
23	8·63	**73**	27·38	**123**	46·13	**173**	64·88	**223**	83·63	**273**	102·38	**323**	121·13	**373**	139·88	**423**	158·63	**473**	177·38
24	9·00	**74**	27·75	**124**	46·50	**174**	65·25	**224**	84·00	**274**	102·75	**324**	121·50	**374**	140·25	**424**	159·00	**474**	177·75
25	9·38	**75**	28·13	**125**	46·88	**175**	65·63	**225**	84·38	**275**	103·13	**325**	121·88	**375**	140·63	**425**	159·38	**475**	178·13
26	9·75	**76**	28·50	**126**	47·25	**176**	66·00	**226**	84·75	**276**	103·50	**326**	122·25	**376**	141·00	**426**	159·75	**476**	178·50
27	10·13	**77**	28·88	**127**	47·63	**177**	66·38	**227**	85·13	**277**	103·88	**327**	122·63	**377**	141·38	**427**	160·13	**477**	178·88
28	10·50	**78**	29·25	**128**	48·00	**178**	66·75	**228**	85·50	**278**	104·25	**328**	123·00	**378**	141·75	**428**	160·50	**478**	179·25
29	10·88	**79**	29·63	**129**	48·38	**179**	67·13	**229**	85·88	**279**	104·63	**329**	123·38	**379**	142·13	**429**	160·88	**479**	179·63
30	11·25	**80**	30·00	**130**	48·75	**180**	67·50	**230**	86·25	**280**	105·00	**330**	123·75	**380**	142·50	**430**	161·25	**480**	180·00
31	11·63	**81**	30·38	**131**	49·13	**181**	67·88	**231**	86·63	**281**	105·38	**331**	124·13	**381**	142·88	**431**	161·63	**481**	180·38
32	12·00	**82**	30·75	**132**	49·50	**182**	68·25	**232**	87·00	**282**	105·75	**332**	124·50	**382**	143·25	**432**	162·00	**482**	180·75
33	12·38	**83**	31·13	**133**	49·88	**183**	68·63	**233**	87·38	**283**	106·13	**333**	124·88	**383**	143·63	**433**	162·38	**483**	181·13
34	12·75	**84**	31·50	**134**	50·25	**184**	69·00	**234**	87·75	**284**	106·50	**334**	125·25	**384**	144·00	**434**	162·75	**484**	181·50
35	13·13	**85**	31·88	**135**	50·63	**185**	69·38	**235**	88·13	**285**	106·88	**335**	125·63	**385**	144·38	**435**	163·13	**485**	181·88
36	13·50	**86**	32·25	**136**	51·00	**186**	69·75	**236**	88·50	**286**	107·25	**336**	126·00	**386**	144·75	**436**	163·50	**486**	182·25
37	13·88	**87**	32·63	**137**	51·38	**187**	70·13	**237**	88·88	**287**	107·63	**337**	126·38	**387**	145·13	**437**	163·88	**487**	182·63
38	14·25	**88**	33·00	**138**	51·75	**188**	70·50	**238**	89·25	**288**	108·00	**338**	126·75	**388**	145·50	**438**	164·25	**488**	183·00
39	14·63	**89**	33·38	**139**	52·13	**189**	70·88	**239**	89·63	**289**	108·38	**339**	127·13	**389**	145·88	**439**	164·63	**489**	183·38
40	15·00	**90**	33·75	**140**	52·50	**190**	71·25	**240**	90·00	**290**	108·75	**340**	127·50	**390**	146·25	**440**	165·00	**490**	183·75
41	15·38	**91**	34·13	**141**	52·88	**191**	71·63	**241**	90·38	**291**	109·13	**341**	127·88	**391**	146·63	**441**	165·38	**491**	184·13
42	15·75	**92**	34·50	**142**	53·25	**192**	72·00	**242**	90·75	**292**	109·50	**342**	128·25	**392**	147·00	**442**	165·75	**492**	184·50
43	16·13	**93**	34·88	**143**	53·63	**193**	72·38	**243**	91·13	**293**	109·88	**343**	128·63	**393**	147·38	**443**	166·13	**493**	184·88
44	16·50	**94**	35·25	**144**	54·00	**194**	72·75	**244**	91·50	**294**	110·25	**344**	129·00	**394**	147·75	**444**	166·50	**494**	185·25
45	16·88	**95**	35·63	**145**	54·38	**195**	73·13	**245**	91·88	**295**	110·63	**345**	129·38	**395**	148·13	**445**	166·88	**495**	185·63
46	17·25	**96**	36·00	**146**	54·75	**196**	73·50	**246**	92·25	**296**	111·00	**346**	129·75	**396**	148·50	**446**	167·25	**496**	186·00
47	17·63	**97**	36·38	**147**	55·13	**197**	73·88	**247**	92·63	**297**	111·38	**347**	130·13	**397**	148·88	**447**	167·63	**497**	186·38
48	18·00	**98**	36·75	**148**	55·50	**198**	74·25	**248**	93·00	**298**	111·75	**348**	130·50	**398**	149·25	**448**	168·00	**498**	186·75
49	18·38	**99**	37·13	**149**	55·88	**199**	74·63	**249**	93·38	**299**	112·13	**349**	130·88	**399**	149·63	**449**	168·38	**499**	187·13
50	18·75	**100**	37·50	**150**	56·25	**200**	75·00	**250**	93·75	**300**	112·50	**350**	131·25	**400**	150·00	**450**	168·75	**500**	187·50
On Tax		**£1,000** £375		**£1,500** £563		**£2,000** £750		**£2,500** £938		**£3,000** £1,125		**£3,500** £1,313		**£4,000** £1,500		**£4,500** £1,688		**£5,000** £1,875	

38.1% 2018/19 and 2019/20: Income Tax on Dividend Income

Payable by additional rate taxpayers on dividends exceeding the dividend allowance
(Note: The dividend allowance has been reduced from £5,000 to £2,000 for 2018/19 onwards).

£ or p	Tax £ or p	£ or p	Tax £ or p	£	Tax £	£	Tax £	£	Tax £	£	Tax £	£	Tax £	£	Tax £	£	Tax £	£	Tax £
1	0·38	**51**	19·43	**101**	38·48	**151**	57·53	**201**	76·58	**251**	95·63	**301**	114·68	**351**	133·73	**401**	152·78	**451**	171·83
2	0·76	**52**	19·81	**102**	38·86	**152**	57·91	**202**	76·96	**252**	96·01	**302**	115·06	**352**	134·11	**402**	153·16	**452**	172·21
3	1·14	**53**	20·19	**103**	39·24	**153**	58·29	**203**	77·34	**253**	96·39	**303**	115·44	**353**	134·49	**403**	153·54	**453**	172·59
4	1·52	**54**	20·57	**104**	39·62	**154**	58·67	**204**	77·72	**254**	96·77	**304**	115·82	**354**	134·87	**404**	153·92	**454**	172·97
5	1·91	**55**	20·96	**105**	40·01	**155**	59·06	**205**	78·11	**255**	97·16	**305**	116·21	**355**	135·26	**405**	154·31	**455**	173·36
6	2·29	**56**	21·34	**106**	40·39	**156**	59·44	**206**	78·49	**256**	97·54	**306**	116·59	**356**	135·64	**406**	154·69	**456**	173·74
7	2·67	**57**	21·72	**107**	40·77	**157**	59·82	**207**	78·87	**257**	97·92	**307**	116·97	**357**	136·02	**407**	155·07	**457**	174·12
8	3·05	**58**	22·10	**108**	41·15	**158**	60·20	**208**	79·25	**258**	98·30	**308**	117·35	**358**	136·40	**408**	155·45	**458**	174·50
9	3·43	**59**	22·48	**109**	41·53	**159**	60·58	**209**	79·63	**259**	98·68	**309**	117·73	**359**	136·78	**409**	155·83	**459**	174·88
10	3·81	**60**	22·86	**110**	41·91	**160**	60·96	**210**	80·01	**260**	99·06	**310**	118·11	**360**	137·16	**410**	156·21	**460**	175·26
11	4·19	**61**	23·24	**111**	42·29	**161**	61·34	**211**	80·39	**261**	99·44	**311**	118·49	**361**	137·54	**411**	156·59	**461**	175·64
12	4·57	**62**	23·62	**112**	42·67	**162**	61·72	**212**	80·77	**262**	99·82	**312**	118·87	**362**	137·92	**412**	156·97	**462**	176·02
13	4·95	**63**	24·00	**113**	43·05	**163**	62·10	**213**	81·15	**263**	100·20	**313**	119·25	**363**	138·30	**413**	157·35	**463**	176·40
14	5·33	**64**	24·38	**114**	43·43	**164**	62·48	**214**	81·53	**264**	100·58	**314**	119·63	**364**	138·68	**414**	157·73	**464**	176·78
15	5·72	**65**	24·77	**115**	43·82	**165**	62·87	**215**	81·92	**265**	100·97	**315**	120·02	**365**	139·07	**415**	158·12	**465**	177·17
16	6·10	**66**	25·15	**116**	44·20	**166**	63·25	**216**	82·30	**266**	101·35	**316**	120·40	**366**	139·45	**416**	158·50	**466**	177·55
17	6·48	**67**	25·53	**117**	44·58	**167**	63·63	**217**	82·68	**267**	101·73	**317**	120·78	**367**	139·83	**417**	158·88	**467**	177·93
18	6·86	**68**	25·91	**118**	44·96	**168**	64·01	**218**	83·06	**268**	102·11	**318**	121·16	**368**	140·21	**418**	159·26	**468**	178·31
19	7·24	**69**	26·29	**119**	45·34	**169**	64·39	**219**	83·44	**269**	102·49	**319**	121·54	**369**	140·59	**419**	159·64	**469**	178·69
20	7·62	**70**	26·67	**120**	45·72	**170**	64·77	**220**	83·82	**270**	102·87	**320**	121·92	**370**	140·97	**420**	160·02	**470**	179·07
21	8·00	**71**	27·05	**121**	46·10	**171**	65·15	**221**	84·20	**271**	103·25	**321**	122·30	**371**	141·35	**421**	160·40	**471**	179·45
22	8·38	**72**	27·43	**122**	46·48	**172**	65·53	**222**	84·58	**272**	103·63	**322**	122·68	**372**	141·73	**422**	160·78	**472**	179·83
23	8·76	**73**	27·81	**123**	46·86	**173**	65·91	**223**	84·96	**273**	104·01	**323**	123·06	**373**	142·11	**423**	161·16	**473**	180·21
24	9·14	**74**	28·19	**124**	47·24	**174**	66·29	**224**	85·34	**274**	104·39	**324**	123·44	**374**	142·49	**424**	161·54	**474**	180·59
25	9·53	**75**	28·58	**125**	47·63	**175**	66·68	**225**	85·73	**275**	104·78	**325**	123·83	**375**	142·88	**425**	161·93	**475**	180·98
26	9·91	**76**	28·96	**126**	48·01	**176**	67·06	**226**	86·11	**276**	105·16	**326**	124·21	**376**	143·26	**426**	162·31	**476**	181·36
27	10·29	**77**	29·34	**127**	48·39	**177**	67·44	**227**	86·49	**277**	105·54	**327**	124·59	**377**	143·64	**427**	162·69	**477**	181·74
28	10·67	**78**	29·72	**128**	48·77	**178**	67·82	**228**	86·87	**278**	105·92	**328**	124·97	**378**	144·02	**428**	163·07	**478**	182·12
29	11·05	**79**	30·10	**129**	49·15	**179**	68·20	**229**	87·25	**279**	106·30	**329**	125·35	**379**	144·40	**429**	163·45	**479**	182·50
30	11·43	**80**	30·48	**130**	49·53	**180**	68·58	**230**	87·63	**280**	106·68	**330**	125·73	**380**	144·78	**430**	163·83	**480**	182·88
31	11·81	**81**	30·86	**131**	49·91	**181**	68·96	**231**	88·01	**281**	107·06	**331**	126·11	**381**	145·16	**431**	164·21	**481**	183·26
32	12·19	**82**	31·24	**132**	50·29	**182**	69·34	**232**	88·39	**282**	107·44	**332**	126·49	**382**	145·54	**432**	164·59	**482**	183·64
33	12·57	**83**	31·62	**133**	50·67	**183**	69·72	**233**	88·77	**283**	107·82	**333**	126·87	**383**	145·92	**433**	164·97	**483**	184·02
34	12·95	**84**	32·00	**134**	51·05	**184**	70·10	**234**	89·15	**284**	108·20	**334**	127·25	**384**	146·30	**434**	165·35	**484**	184·40
35	13·34	**85**	32·39	**135**	51·44	**185**	70·49	**235**	89·54	**285**	108·59	**335**	127·64	**385**	146·69	**435**	165·74	**485**	184·79
36	13·72	**86**	32·77	**136**	51·82	**186**	70·87	**236**	89·92	**286**	108·97	**336**	128·02	**386**	147·07	**436**	166·12	**486**	185·17
37	14·10	**87**	33·15	**137**	52·20	**187**	71·25	**237**	90·30	**287**	109·35	**337**	128·40	**387**	147·45	**437**	166·50	**487**	185·55
38	14·48	**88**	33·53	**138**	52·58	**188**	71·63	**238**	90·68	**288**	109·73	**338**	128·78	**388**	147·83	**438**	166·88	**488**	185·93
39	14·86	**89**	33·91	**139**	52·96	**189**	72·01	**239**	91·06	**289**	110·11	**339**	129·16	**389**	148·21	**439**	167·26	**489**	186·31
40	15·24	**90**	34·29	**140**	53·34	**190**	72·39	**240**	91·44	**290**	110·49	**340**	129·54	**390**	148·59	**440**	167·64	**490**	186·69
41	15·62	**91**	34·67	**141**	53·72	**191**	72·77	**241**	91·82	**291**	110·87	**341**	129·92	**391**	148·97	**441**	168·02	**491**	187·07
42	16·00	**92**	35·05	**142**	54·10	**192**	73·15	**242**	92·20	**292**	111·25	**342**	130·30	**392**	149·35	**442**	168·40	**492**	187·45
43	16·38	**93**	35·43	**143**	54·48	**193**	73·53	**243**	92·58	**293**	111·63	**343**	130·68	**393**	149·73	**443**	168·78	**493**	187·83
44	16·76	**94**	35·81	**144**	54·86	**194**	73·91	**244**	92·96	**294**	112·01	**344**	131·06	**394**	150·11	**444**	169·16	**494**	188·21
45	17·15	**95**	36·20	**145**	55·25	**195**	74·30	**245**	93·35	**295**	112·40	**345**	131·45	**395**	150·50	**445**	169·55	**495**	188·60
46	17·53	**96**	36·58	**146**	55·63	**196**	74·68	**246**	93·73	**296**	112·78	**346**	131·83	**396**	150·88	**446**	169·93	**496**	188·98
47	17·91	**97**	36·96	**147**	56·01	**197**	75·06	**247**	94·11	**297**	113·16	**347**	132·21	**397**	151·26	**447**	170·31	**497**	189·36
48	18·29	**98**	37·34	**148**	56·39	**198**	75·44	**248**	94·49	**298**	113·54	**348**	132·59	**398**	151·64	**448**	170·69	**498**	189·74
49	18·67	**99**	37·72	**149**	56·77	**199**	75·82	**249**	94·87	**299**	113·92	**349**	132·97	**399**	152·02	**449**	171·07	**499**	190·12
50	19·05	**100**	38·10	**150**	57·15	**200**	76·20	**250**	95·25	**300**	114·30	**350**	133·35	**400**	152·40	**450**	171·45	**500**	190·50

On	**£1,000**	**£1,500**	**£2,000**	**£2,500**	**£3,000**	**£3,500**	**£4,000**	**£4,500**	**£5,000**
Tax	£381·00	£571·50	£762·00	£952·50	£1,143·00	£1,333·50	£1,524·00	£1,714·50	£1,905

Payable by additional rate taxpayers on dividends exceeding the dividend allowance
(Note: The dividend allowance has been reduced from £5,000 to £2,000 for 2018/19 onwards).

2018/19 and 2019/20: Income Tax on Dividend Income 38.1%

£ or p	Tax £ or p	£ or p	Tax £ or p	£	Tax £	£	Tax £	£	Tax £	£	Tax £	£	Tax £	£	Tax £	£	Tax £	£	Tax £
501	190·88	**551**	209·93	**601**	228·98	**651**	248·03	**701**	267·08	**751**	286·13	**801**	305·18	**851**	324·23	**901**	343·28	**951**	362·33
502	191·26	**552**	210·31	**602**	229·36	**652**	248·41	**702**	267·46	**752**	286·51	**802**	305·56	**852**	324·61	**902**	343·66	**952**	362·71
503	191·64	**553**	210·69	**603**	229·74	**653**	248·79	**703**	267·84	**753**	286·89	**803**	305·94	**853**	324·99	**903**	344·04	**953**	363·09
504	192·02	**554**	211·07	**604**	230·12	**654**	249·17	**704**	268·22	**754**	287·27	**804**	306·32	**854**	325·37	**904**	344·42	**954**	363·47
505	192·41	**555**	211·46	**605**	230·51	**655**	249·56	**705**	268·61	**755**	287·66	**805**	306·71	**855**	325·76	**905**	344·81	**955**	363·86
506	192·79	**556**	211·84	**606**	230·89	**656**	249·94	**706**	268·99	**756**	288·04	**806**	307·09	**856**	326·14	**906**	345·19	**956**	364·24
507	193·17	**557**	212·22	**607**	231·27	**657**	250·32	**707**	269·37	**757**	288·42	**807**	307·47	**857**	326·52	**907**	345·57	**957**	364·62
508	193·55	**558**	212·60	**608**	231·65	**658**	250·70	**708**	269·75	**758**	288·80	**808**	307·85	**858**	326·90	**908**	345·95	**958**	365·00
509	193·93	**559**	212·98	**609**	232·03	**659**	251·08	**709**	270·13	**759**	289·18	**809**	308·23	**859**	327·28	**909**	346·33	**959**	365·38
510	194·31	**560**	213·36	**610**	232·41	**660**	251·46	**710**	270·51	**760**	289·56	**810**	308·61	**860**	327·66	**910**	346·71	**960**	365·76
511	194·69	**561**	213·74	**611**	232·79	**661**	251·84	**711**	270·89	**761**	289·94	**811**	308·99	**861**	328·04	**911**	347·09	**961**	366·14
512	195·07	**562**	214·12	**612**	233·17	**662**	252·22	**712**	271·27	**762**	290·32	**812**	309·37	**862**	328·42	**912**	347·47	**962**	366·52
513	195·45	**563**	214·50	**613**	233·55	**663**	252·60	**713**	271·65	**763**	290·70	**813**	309·75	**863**	328·80	**913**	347·85	**963**	366·90
514	195·83	**564**	214·88	**614**	233·93	**664**	252·98	**714**	272·03	**764**	291·08	**814**	310·13	**864**	329·18	**914**	348·23	**964**	367·28
515	196·22	**565**	215·27	**615**	234·32	**665**	253·37	**715**	272·42	**765**	291·47	**815**	310·52	**865**	329·57	**915**	348·62	**965**	367·67
516	196·60	**566**	215·65	**616**	234·70	**666**	253·75	**716**	272·80	**766**	291·85	**816**	310·90	**866**	329·95	**916**	349·00	**966**	368·05
517	196·98	**567**	216·03	**617**	235·08	**667**	254·13	**717**	273·18	**767**	292·23	**817**	311·28	**867**	330·33	**917**	349·38	**967**	368·43
518	197·36	**568**	216·41	**618**	235·46	**668**	254·51	**718**	273·56	**768**	292·61	**818**	311·66	**868**	330·71	**918**	349·76	**968**	368·81
519	197·74	**569**	216·79	**619**	235·84	**669**	254·89	**719**	273·94	**769**	292·99	**819**	312·04	**869**	331·09	**919**	350·14	**969**	369·19
520	198·12	**570**	217·17	**620**	236·22	**670**	255·27	**720**	274·32	**770**	293·37	**820**	312·42	**870**	331·47	**920**	350·52	**970**	369·57
521	198·50	**571**	217·55	**621**	236·60	**671**	255·65	**721**	274·70	**771**	293·75	**821**	312·80	**871**	331·85	**921**	350·90	**971**	369·95
522	198·88	**572**	217·93	**622**	236·98	**672**	256·03	**722**	275·08	**772**	294·13	**822**	313·18	**872**	332·23	**922**	351·28	**972**	370·33
523	199·26	**573**	218·31	**623**	237·36	**673**	256·41	**723**	275·46	**773**	294·51	**823**	313·56	**873**	332·61	**923**	351·66	**973**	370·71
524	199·64	**574**	218·69	**624**	237·74	**674**	256·79	**724**	275·84	**774**	294·89	**824**	313·94	**874**	332·99	**924**	352·04	**974**	371·09
525	200·03	**575**	219·08	**625**	238·13	**675**	257·18	**725**	276·23	**775**	295·28	**825**	314·33	**875**	333·38	**925**	352·43	**975**	371·48
526	200·41	**576**	219·46	**626**	238·51	**676**	257·56	**726**	276·61	**776**	295·66	**826**	314·71	**876**	333·76	**926**	352·81	**976**	371·86
527	200·79	**577**	219·84	**627**	238·89	**677**	257·94	**727**	276·99	**777**	296·04	**827**	315·09	**877**	334·14	**927**	353·19	**977**	372·24
528	201·17	**578**	220·22	**628**	239·27	**678**	258·32	**728**	277·37	**778**	296·42	**828**	315·47	**878**	334·52	**928**	353·57	**978**	372·62
529	201·55	**579**	220·60	**629**	239·65	**679**	258·70	**729**	277·75	**779**	296·80	**829**	315·85	**879**	334·90	**929**	353·95	**979**	373·00
530	201·93	**580**	220·98	**630**	240·03	**680**	259·08	**730**	278·13	**780**	297·18	**830**	316·23	**880**	335·28	**930**	354·33	**980**	373·38
531	202·31	**581**	221·36	**631**	240·41	**681**	259·46	**731**	278·51	**781**	297·56	**831**	316·61	**881**	335·66	**931**	354·71	**981**	373·76
532	202·69	**582**	221·74	**632**	240·79	**682**	259·84	**732**	278·89	**782**	297·94	**832**	316·99	**882**	336·04	**932**	355·09	**982**	374·14
533	203·07	**583**	222·12	**633**	241·17	**683**	260·22	**733**	279·27	**783**	298·32	**833**	317·37	**883**	336·42	**933**	355·47	**983**	374·52
534	203·45	**584**	222·50	**634**	241·55	**684**	260·60	**734**	279·65	**784**	298·70	**834**	317·75	**884**	336·80	**934**	355·85	**984**	374·90
535	203·84	**585**	222·89	**635**	241·94	**685**	260·99	**735**	280·04	**785**	299·09	**835**	318·14	**885**	337·19	**935**	356·24	**985**	375·29
536	204·22	**586**	223·27	**636**	242·32	**686**	261·37	**736**	280·42	**786**	299·47	**836**	318·52	**886**	337·57	**936**	356·62	**986**	375·67
537	204·60	**587**	223·65	**637**	242·70	**687**	261·75	**737**	280·80	**787**	299·85	**837**	318·90	**887**	337·95	**937**	357·00	**987**	376·05
538	204·98	**588**	224·03	**638**	243·08	**688**	262·13	**738**	281·18	**788**	300·23	**838**	319·28	**888**	338·33	**938**	357·38	**988**	376·43
539	205·36	**589**	224·41	**639**	243·46	**689**	262·51	**739**	281·56	**789**	300·61	**839**	319·66	**889**	338·71	**939**	357·76	**989**	376·81
540	205·74	**590**	224·79	**640**	243·84	**690**	262·89	**740**	281·94	**790**	300·99	**840**	320·04	**890**	339·09	**940**	358·14	**990**	377·19
541	206·12	**591**	225·17	**641**	244·22	**691**	26·29	**741**	282·32	**791**	301·37	**841**	320·42	**891**	339·47	**941**	358·52	**991**	377·57
542	206·50	**592**	225·55	**642**	244·60	**692**	263·65	**742**	282·70	**792**	301·75	**842**	320·80	**892**	339·85	**942**	358·90	**992**	377·95
543	206·88	**593**	225·93	**643**	244·98	**693**	264·03	**743**	283·08	**793**	302·13	**843**	321·18	**893**	340·23	**943**	359·28	**993**	378·33
544	207·26	**594**	226·31	**644**	245·36	**694**	264·41	**744**	283·46	**794**	302·51	**844**	321·56	**894**	340·61	**944**	359·66	**994**	378·71
545	207·65	**595**	226·70	**645**	245·75	**695**	264·80	**745**	283·85	**795**	302·90	**845**	321·95	**895**	341·00	**945**	360·05	**995**	379·10
546	208·03	**596**	227·08	**646**	246·13	**696**	265·18	**746**	284·23	**796**	303·28	**846**	322·33	**896**	341·38	**946**	360·43	**996**	379·48
547	208·41	**597**	227·46	**647**	246·51	**697**	265·56	**747**	284·61	**797**	303·66	**847**	322·71	**897**	341·76	**947**	360·81	**997**	379·86
548	208·79	**598**	227·84	**648**	246·89	**698**	265·94	**748**	284·99	**798**	304·04	**848**	323·09	**898**	342·14	**948**	361·19	**998**	380·24
549	209·17	**599**	228·22	**649**	247·27	**699**	266·32	**749**	285·37	**799**	304·42	**849**	323·47	**899**	342·52	**949**	361·57	**999**	380·62
550	209·55	**600**	228·60	**650**	247·65	**700**	266·70	**750**	285·75	**800**	304·80	**850**	323·85	**900**	342·90	**950**	361·95	**1000**	381·00
On		**£5,500**		**£6,000**		**£6,500**		**£7,000**		**£7,500**		**£8,000**		**£8,500**		**£9,000**		**£9,500**	
Tax		£2,095·50		£2,286·00		£2,476·50		£2,667·00		£2,857·50		£3,048·00		£3,238·50		£3,429·00		£3,619·50	

40% 2018/19 and 2019/20: Income Tax (a) Inheritance Tax (b)

(a) Payable on taxable income between £34,501 (£37,500 for 2019/20) and £150,000.
(b) Payable on chargeable transfers over £325,000. (but note additional nil-rate band of £125,000 for 2018/19 and £150,000 for 2019/20, where residence passed on death to direct descendant).

£ or p	Tax £ or p	£ or p	Tax £ or p	£	Tax £	£	Tax £	£	Tax £	£	Tax £	£	Tax £	£	Tax £	£	Tax £	£	Tax £
1	0·40	**51**	20·40	**101**	40·40	**151**	60·40	**201**	80·40	**251**	100·40	**301**	120·40	**351**	140·40	**401**	160·40	**451**	180·40
2	0·80	**52**	20·80	**102**	40·80	**152**	60·80	**202**	80·80	**252**	100·80	**302**	120·80	**352**	140·80	**402**	160·80	**452**	180·80
3	1·20	**53**	21·20	**103**	41·20	**153**	61·20	**203**	81·20	**253**	101·20	**303**	121·20	**353**	141·20	**403**	161·20	**453**	181·20
4	1·60	**54**	21·60	**104**	41·60	**154**	61·60	**204**	81·60	**254**	101·60	**304**	121·60	**354**	141·60	**404**	161·60	**454**	181·60
5	2·00	**55**	22·00	**105**	42·00	**155**	62·00	**205**	82·00	**255**	102·00	**305**	122·00	**355**	142·00	**405**	162·00	**455**	182·00
6	2·40	**56**	22·40	**106**	42·40	**156**	62·40	**206**	82·40	**256**	102·40	**306**	122·40	**356**	142·40	**406**	162·40	**456**	182·40
7	2·80	**57**	22·80	**107**	42·80	**157**	62·80	**207**	82·80	**257**	102·80	**307**	122·80	**357**	142·80	**407**	162·80	**457**	182·80
8	3·20	**58**	23·20	**108**	43·20	**158**	63·20	**208**	83·20	**258**	103·20	**308**	123·20	**358**	143·20	**408**	163·20	**458**	183·20
9	3·60	**59**	23·60	**109**	43·60	**159**	63·60	**209**	83·60	**259**	103·60	**309**	123·60	**359**	143·60	**409**	163·60	**459**	183·60
10	4·00	**60**	24·00	**110**	44·00	**160**	64·00	**210**	84·00	**260**	104·00	**310**	124·00	**360**	144·00	**410**	164·00	**460**	184·00
11	4·40	**61**	24·40	**111**	44·40	**161**	64·40	**211**	84·40	**261**	104·40	**311**	124·40	**361**	144·40	**411**	164·40	**461**	184·40
12	4·80	**62**	24·80	**112**	44·80	**162**	64·80	**212**	84·80	**262**	104·80	**312**	124·80	**362**	144·80	**412**	164·80	**462**	184·80
13	5·20	**63**	25·20	**113**	45·20	**163**	65·20	**213**	85·20	**263**	105·20	**313**	125·20	**363**	145·20	**413**	165·20	**463**	185·20
14	5·60	**64**	25·60	**114**	45·60	**164**	65·60	**214**	85·60	**264**	105·60	**314**	125·60	**364**	145·60	**414**	165·60	**464**	185·60
15	6·00	**65**	26·00	**115**	46·00	**165**	66·00	**215**	86·00	**265**	106·00	**315**	126·00	**365**	146·00	**415**	166·00	**465**	186·00
16	6·40	**66**	26·40	**116**	46·40	**166**	66·40	**216**	86·40	**266**	106·40	**316**	126·40	**366**	146·40	**416**	166·40	**466**	186·40
17	6·80	**67**	26·80	**117**	46·80	**167**	66·80	**217**	86·80	**267**	106·80	**317**	126·80	**367**	146·80	**417**	166·80	**467**	186·80
18	7·20	**68**	27·20	**118**	47·20	**168**	67·20	**218**	87·20	**268**	107·20	**318**	127·20	**368**	147·20	**418**	167·20	**468**	187·20
19	7·60	**69**	27·60	**119**	47·60	**169**	67·60	**219**	87·60	**269**	107·60	**319**	127·60	**369**	147·60	**419**	167·60	**469**	187·60
20	8·00	**70**	28·00	**120**	48·00	**170**	68·00	**220**	88·00	**270**	108·00	**320**	128·00	**370**	148·00	**420**	168·00	**470**	188·00
21	8·40	**71**	28·40	**121**	48·40	**171**	68·40	**221**	88·40	**271**	108·40	**321**	128·40	**371**	148·40	**421**	168·40	**471**	188·40
22	8·80	**72**	28·80	**122**	48·80	**172**	68·80	**222**	88·80	**272**	108·80	**322**	128·80	**372**	148·80	**422**	168·80	**472**	188·80
23	9·20	**73**	29·20	**123**	49·20	**173**	69·20	**223**	89·20	**273**	109·20	**323**	129·20	**373**	149·20	**423**	169·20	**473**	189·20
24	9·60	**74**	29·60	**124**	49·60	**174**	69·60	**224**	89·60	**274**	109·60	**324**	129·60	**374**	149·60	**424**	169·60	**474**	189·60
25	10·00	**75**	30·00	**125**	50·00	**175**	70·00	**225**	90·00	**275**	110·00	**325**	130·00	**375**	150·00	**425**	170·00	**475**	190·00
26	10·40	**76**	30·40	**126**	50·40	**176**	70·40	**226**	90·40	**276**	110·40	**326**	130·40	**376**	150·40	**426**	170·40	**476**	190·40
27	10·80	**77**	30·80	**127**	50·80	**177**	70·80	**227**	90·80	**277**	110·80	**327**	130·80	**377**	150·80	**427**	170·80	**477**	190·80
28	11·20	**78**	31·20	**128**	51·20	**178**	71·20	**228**	91·20	**278**	111·20	**328**	131·20	**378**	151·20	**428**	171·20	**478**	191·20
29	11·60	**79**	31·60	**129**	51·60	**179**	71·60	**229**	91·60	**279**	111·60	**329**	131·60	**379**	151·60	**429**	171·60	**479**	191·60
30	12·00	**80**	32·00	**130**	52·00	**180**	72·00	**230**	92·00	**280**	112·00	**330**	132·00	**380**	152·00	**430**	172·00	**480**	192·00
31	12·40	**81**	32·40	**131**	52·40	**181**	72·40	**231**	92·40	**281**	112·40	**331**	132·40	**381**	152·40	**431**	172·40	**481**	192·40
32	12·80	**82**	32·80	**132**	52·80	**182**	72·80	**232**	92·80	**282**	112·80	**332**	132·80	**382**	152·80	**432**	172·80	**482**	192·80
33	13·20	**83**	33·20	**133**	53·20	**183**	73·20	**233**	93·20	**283**	113·20	**333**	133·20	**383**	153·20	**433**	173·20	**483**	193·20
34	13·60	**84**	33·60	**134**	53·60	**184**	73·60	**234**	93·60	**284**	113·60	**334**	133·60	**384**	153·60	**434**	173·60	**484**	193·60
35	14·00	**85**	34·00	**135**	54·00	**185**	74·00	**235**	94·00	**285**	114·00	**335**	134·00	**385**	154·00	**435**	174·00	**485**	194·00
36	14·40	**86**	34·40	**136**	54·40	**186**	74·40	**236**	94·40	**286**	114·40	**336**	134·40	**386**	154·40	**436**	174·40	**486**	194·40
37	14·80	**87**	34·80	**137**	54·80	**187**	74·80	**237**	94·80	**287**	114·80	**337**	134·80	**387**	154·80	**437**	174·80	**487**	194·80
38	15·20	**88**	35·20	**138**	55·20	**188**	75·20	**238**	95·20	**288**	115·20	**338**	135·20	**388**	155·20	**438**	175·20	**488**	195·20
39	15·60	**89**	35·60	**139**	55·60	**189**	75·60	**239**	95·60	**289**	115·60	**339**	135·60	**389**	155·60	**439**	175·60	**489**	195·60
40	16·00	**90**	36·00	**140**	56·00	**190**	76·00	**240**	96·00	**290**	116·00	**340**	136·00	**390**	156·00	**440**	176·00	**490**	196·00
41	16·40	**91**	36·40	**141**	56·40	**191**	76·40	**241**	96·40	**291**	116·40	**341**	136·40	**391**	156·40	**441**	176·40	**491**	196·40
42	16·80	**92**	36·80	**142**	56·80	**192**	76·80	**242**	96·80	**292**	116·80	**342**	136·80	**392**	156·80	**442**	176·80	**492**	196·80
43	17·20	**93**	37·20	**143**	57·20	**193**	77·20	**243**	97·20	**293**	117·20	**343**	137·20	**393**	157·20	**443**	177·20	**493**	197·20
44	17·60	**94**	37·60	**144**	57·60	**194**	77·60	**244**	97·60	**294**	117·60	**344**	137·60	**394**	157·60	**444**	177·60	**494**	197·60
45	18·00	**95**	38·00	**145**	58·00	**195**	78·00	**245**	98·00	**295**	118·00	**345**	138·00	**395**	158·00	**445**	178·00	**495**	198·00
46	18·40	**96**	38·40	**146**	58·40	**196**	78·40	**246**	98·40	**296**	118·40	**346**	138·40	**396**	158·40	**446**	178·40	**496**	198·40
47	18·80	**97**	38·80	**147**	58·80	**197**	78·80	**247**	98·80	**297**	118·80	**347**	138·80	**397**	158·80	**447**	178·80	**497**	198·80
48	19·20	**98**	39·20	**148**	59·20	**198**	79·20	**248**	99·20	**298**	119·20	**348**	139·20	**398**	159·20	**448**	179·20	**498**	199·20
49	19·60	**99**	39·60	**149**	59·60	**199**	79·60	**249**	99·60	**299**	119·60	**349**	139·60	**399**	159·60	**449**	179·60	**499**	199·60
50	20·00	**100**	40·00	**150**	60·00	**200**	80·00	**250**	100·00	**300**	120·00	**350**	140·00	**400**	160·00	**450**	180·00	**500**	200·00
On Tax		**£1,000** £400		**£1,500** £600		**£2,000** £800		**£2,500** £1,000		**£3,000** £1,200		**£3,500** £1,400		**£4,000** £1,600		**£4,500** £1,800		**£5,000** £2,000	

(a) Additional rate payable on taxable income over £150,000.
(b) Trust rate

2018/19 and 2019/20: Income Tax (a) Trusts (b) 45%

£ or p	Tax £ or p	£ or p	Tax £ or p	£	Tax £	£	Tax £	£	Tax £	£	Tax £	£	Tax £	£	Tax £	£	Tax £	£	Tax £
1	0·45	**51**	22·95	**101**	45·45	**151**	67·95	**201**	90·45	**251**	112·95	**301**	135·45	**351**	157·95	**401**	180·45	**451**	202·95
2	0·90	**52**	23·40	**102**	45·90	**152**	68·40	**202**	90·90	**252**	113·40	**302**	135·90	**352**	158·40	**402**	180·90	**452**	203·40
3	1·35	**53**	23·85	**103**	46·35	**153**	68·85	**203**	91·35	**253**	113·85	**303**	136·35	**353**	158·85	**403**	181·35	**453**	203·85
4	1·80	**54**	24·30	**104**	46·80	**154**	69·30	**204**	91·80	**254**	114·30	**304**	136·80	**354**	159·30	**404**	181·80	**454**	204·30
5	2·25	**55**	24·75	**105**	47·25	**155**	69·75	**205**	92·25	**255**	114·75	**305**	137·25	**355**	159·75	**405**	182·25	**455**	204·75
6	2·70	**56**	25·20	**106**	47·70	**156**	70·20	**206**	92·70	**256**	115·20	**306**	137·70	**356**	160·20	**406**	182·70	**456**	205·20
7	3·15	**57**	25·65	**107**	48·15	**157**	70·65	**207**	93·15	**257**	115·65	**307**	138·15	**357**	160·65	**407**	183·15	**457**	205·65
8	3·60	**58**	26·10	**108**	48·60	**158**	71·10	**208**	93·60	**258**	116·10	**308**	138·60	**358**	161·10	**408**	183·60	**458**	206·10
9	4·05	**59**	26·55	**109**	49·05	**159**	71·55	**209**	94·05	**259**	116·55	**309**	139·05	**359**	161·55	**409**	184·05	**459**	206·55
10	4·50	**60**	27·00	**110**	49·50	**160**	72·00	**210**	94·50	**260**	117·00	**310**	139·50	**360**	162·00	**410**	184·50	**460**	207·00
11	4·95	**61**	27·45	**111**	49·95	**161**	72·45	**211**	94·95	**261**	117·45	**311**	139·95	**361**	162·45	**411**	184·95	**461**	207·45
12	5·40	**62**	27·90	**112**	50·40	**162**	72·90	**212**	95·40	**262**	117·90	**312**	140·40	**362**	162·90	**412**	185·40	**462**	207·90
13	5·85	**63**	28·35	**113**	50·85	**163**	73·35	**213**	95·85	**263**	118·35	**313**	140·85	**363**	163·35	**413**	185·85	**463**	208·35
14	6·30	**64**	28·80	**114**	51·30	**164**	73·80	**214**	96·30	**264**	118·80	**314**	141·30	**364**	163·80	**414**	186·30	**464**	208·80
15	6·75	**65**	29·25	**115**	51·75	**165**	74·25	**215**	96·75	**265**	119·25	**315**	141·75	**365**	164·25	**415**	186·75	**465**	209·25
16	7·20	**66**	29·70	**116**	52·20	**166**	74·70	**216**	97·20	**266**	119·70	**316**	142·20	**366**	164·70	**416**	187·20	**466**	209·70
17	7·65	**67**	30·15	**117**	52·65	**167**	75·15	**217**	97·65	**267**	120·15	**317**	142·65	**367**	165·15	**417**	187·65	**467**	210·15
18	8·10	**68**	30·60	**118**	53·10	**168**	75·60	**218**	98·10	**268**	120·60	**318**	143·10	**368**	165·60	**418**	188·10	**468**	210·60
19	8·55	**69**	31·05	**119**	53·55	**169**	76·05	**219**	98·55	**269**	121·05	**319**	143·55	**369**	166·05	**419**	188·55	**469**	211·05
20	9·00	**70**	31·50	**120**	54·00	**170**	76·50	**220**	99·00	**270**	121·50	**320**	144·00	**370**	166·50	**420**	189·00	**470**	211·50
21	9·45	**71**	31·95	**121**	54·45	**171**	76·95	**221**	99·45	**271**	121·95	**321**	144·45	**371**	166·95	**421**	189·45	**471**	211·95
22	9·90	**72**	32·40	**122**	54·90	**172**	77·40	**222**	99·90	**272**	122·40	**322**	144·90	**372**	167·40	**422**	189·90	**472**	212·40
23	10·35	**73**	32·85	**123**	55·35	**173**	77·85	**223**	100·35	**273**	122·85	**323**	145·35	**373**	167·85	**423**	190·35	**473**	212·85
24	10·80	**74**	33·30	**124**	55·80	**174**	78·30	**224**	100·80	**274**	123·30	**324**	145·80	**374**	168·30	**424**	190·80	**474**	213·30
25	11·25	**75**	33·75	**125**	56·25	**175**	78·75	**225**	101·25	**275**	123·75	**325**	146·25	**375**	168·75	**425**	191·25	**475**	213·75
26	11·70	**76**	34·20	**126**	56·70	**176**	79·20	**226**	101·70	**276**	124·20	**326**	146·70	**376**	169·20	**426**	191·70	**476**	214·20
27	12·15	**77**	34·65	**127**	57·15	**177**	79·65	**227**	102·15	**277**	124·65	**327**	147·15	**377**	169·65	**427**	192·15	**477**	214·65
28	12·60	**78**	35·10	**128**	57·60	**178**	80·10	**228**	102·60	**278**	125·10	**328**	147·60	**378**	170·10	**428**	192·60	**478**	215·10
29	13·05	**79**	35·55	**129**	58·05	**179**	80·55	**229**	103·05	**279**	125·55	**329**	148·05	**379**	170·55	**429**	193·05	**479**	215·55
30	13·50	**80**	36·00	**130**	58·50	**180**	81·00	**230**	103·50	**280**	126·00	**330**	148·50	**380**	171·00	**430**	193·50	**480**	216·00
31	13·95	**81**	36·45	**131**	58·95	**181**	81·45	**231**	103·95	**281**	126·45	**331**	148·95	**381**	171·45	**431**	193·95	**481**	216·45
32	14·40	**82**	36·90	**132**	59·40	**182**	81·90	**232**	104·40	**282**	126·90	**332**	149·40	**382**	171·90	**432**	194·40	**482**	216·90
33	14·85	**83**	37·35	**133**	59·85	**183**	82·35	**233**	104·85	**283**	127·35	**333**	149·85	**383**	172·35	**433**	194·85	**483**	217·35
34	15·30	**84**	37·80	**134**	60·30	**184**	82·80	**234**	105·30	**284**	127·80	**334**	150·30	**384**	172·80	**434**	195·30	**484**	217·80
35	15·75	**85**	38·25	**135**	60·75	**185**	83·25	**235**	105·75	**285**	128·25	**335**	150·75	**385**	173·25	**435**	195·75	**485**	218·25
36	16·20	**86**	38·70	**136**	61·20	**186**	83·70	**236**	106·20	**286**	128·70	**336**	151·20	**386**	173·70	**436**	196·20	**486**	218·70
37	16·65	**87**	39·15	**137**	61·65	**187**	84·15	**237**	106·65	**287**	129·15	**337**	151·65	**387**	174·15	**437**	196·65	**487**	219·15
38	17·10	**88**	39·60	**138**	62·10	**188**	84·60	**238**	107·10	**288**	129·60	**338**	152·10	**388**	174·60	**438**	197·10	**488**	219·60
39	17·55	**89**	40·05	**139**	62·55	**189**	85·05	**239**	107·55	**289**	130·05	**339**	152·55	**389**	175·05	**439**	197·55	**489**	220·05
40	18·00	**90**	40·50	**140**	63·00	**190**	85·50	**240**	108·00	**290**	130·50	**340**	153·00	**390**	175·50	**440**	198·00	**490**	220·50
41	18·45	**91**	40·95	**141**	63·45	**191**	85·95	**241**	108·45	**291**	130·95	**341**	153·45	**391**	175·95	**441**	198·45	**491**	220·95
42	18·90	**92**	41·40	**142**	63·90	**192**	86·40	**242**	108·90	**292**	131·40	**342**	153·90	**392**	176·40	**442**	198·90	**492**	221·40
43	19·35	**93**	41·85	**143**	64·35	**193**	86·85	**243**	109·35	**293**	131·85	**343**	154·35	**393**	176·85	**443**	199·35	**493**	221·85
44	19·80	**94**	42·30	**144**	64·80	**194**	87·30	**244**	109·80	**294**	132·30	**344**	154·80	**394**	177·30	**444**	199·80	**494**	222·30
45	20·25	**95**	42·75	**145**	65·25	**195**	87·75	**245**	110·25	**295**	132·75	**345**	155·25	**395**	177·75	**445**	200·25	**495**	222·75
46	20·70	**96**	43·20	**146**	65·70	**196**	88·20	**246**	110·70	**296**	133·20	**346**	155·70	**396**	178·20	**446**	200·70	**496**	223·20
47	21·15	**97**	43·65	**147**	66·15	**197**	88·65	**247**	111·15	**297**	133·65	**347**	156·15	**397**	178·65	**447**	201·15	**497**	223·65
48	21·60	**98**	44·10	**148**	66·60	**198**	89·10	**248**	111·60	**298**	134·10	**348**	156·60	**398**	179·10	**448**	201·60	**498**	224·10
49	22·05	**99**	44·55	**149**	67·05	**199**	89·55	**249**	112·05	**299**	134·55	**349**	157·05	**399**	179·55	**449**	202·05	**499**	224·55
50	22·50	**100**	45·00	**150**	67·50	**200**	90·00	**250**	112·50	**300**	135·00	**350**	157·50	**400**	180·00	**450**	202·50	**500**	225·00
On		**£1,000**		**£1,500**		**£2,000**		**£2,500**		**£3,000**		**£3,500**		**£4,000**		**£4,500**		**£5,000**	
Tax		£450		£675		£900		£1,125		£1,350		£1,575		£1,800		£2,025		£2,250	

20% VAT at Standard Rate

£ or p	Tax £ or p	£ or p	Tax £ or p	£	Tax £	£	Tax £	£	Tax £	£	Tax £	£	Tax £	£	Tax £	£	Tax £	£	Tax £
1	0·20	**51**	10·20	**101**	20·20	**151**	30·20	**201**	40·20	**251**	50·20	**301**	60·20	**351**	70·20	**401**	80·20	**451**	90·20
2	0·40	**52**	10·40	**102**	20·40	**152**	30·40	**202**	40·40	**252**	50·40	**302**	60·40	**352**	70·40	**402**	80·40	**452**	90·40
3	0·60	**53**	10·60	**103**	20·60	**153**	30·60	**203**	40·60	**253**	50·60	**303**	60·60	**353**	70·60	**403**	80·60	**453**	90·60
4	0·80	**54**	10·80	**104**	20·80	**154**	30·80	**204**	40·80	**254**	50·80	**304**	60·80	**354**	70·80	**404**	80·80	**454**	90·80
5	1·00	**55**	11·00	**105**	21·00	**155**	31·00	**205**	41·00	**255**	51·00	**305**	61·00	**355**	71·00	**405**	81·00	**455**	91·00
6	1·20	**56**	11·20	**106**	21·20	**156**	31·20	**206**	41·20	**256**	51·20	**306**	61·20	**356**	71·20	**406**	81·20	**456**	91·20
7	1·40	**57**	11·40	**107**	21·40	**157**	31·40	**207**	41·40	**257**	51·40	**307**	61·40	**357**	71·40	**407**	81·40	**457**	91·40
8	1·60	**58**	11·60	**108**	21·60	**158**	31·60	**208**	41·60	**258**	51·60	**308**	61·60	**358**	71·60	**408**	81·60	**458**	91·60
9	1·80	**59**	11·80	**109**	21·80	**159**	31·80	**209**	41·80	**259**	51·80	**309**	61·80	**359**	71·80	**409**	81·80	**459**	91·80
10	2·00	**60**	12·00	**110**	22·00	**160**	32·00	**210**	42·00	**260**	52·00	**310**	62·00	**360**	72·00	**410**	82·00	**460**	92·00
11	2·20	**61**	12·20	**111**	22·20	**161**	32·20	**211**	42·20	**261**	52·20	**311**	62·20	**361**	72·20	**411**	82·20	**461**	92·20
12	2·40	**62**	12·40	**112**	22·40	**162**	32·40	**212**	42·40	**262**	52·40	**312**	62·40	**362**	72·40	**412**	82·40	**462**	92·40
13	2·60	**63**	12·60	**113**	22·60	**163**	32·60	**213**	42·60	**263**	52·60	**313**	62·60	**363**	72·60	**413**	82·60	**463**	92·60
14	2·80	**64**	12·80	**114**	22·80	**164**	32·80	**214**	42·80	**264**	52·80	**314**	62·80	**364**	72·80	**414**	82·80	**464**	92·80
15	3·00	**65**	13·00	**115**	23·00	**165**	33·00	**215**	43·00	**265**	53·00	**315**	63·00	**365**	73·00	**415**	83·00	**465**	93·00
16	3·20	**66**	13·20	**116**	23·20	**166**	33·20	**216**	43·20	**266**	53·20	**316**	63·20	**366**	73·20	**416**	83·20	**466**	93·20
17	3·40	**67**	13·40	**117**	23·40	**167**	33·40	**217**	43·40	**267**	53·40	**317**	63·40	**367**	73·40	**417**	83·40	**467**	93·40
18	3·60	**68**	13·60	**118**	23·60	**168**	33·60	**218**	43·60	**268**	53·60	**318**	63·60	**368**	73·60	**418**	83·60	**468**	93·60
19	3·80	**69**	13·80	**119**	23·80	**169**	33·80	**219**	43·80	**269**	53·80	**319**	63·80	**369**	73·80	**419**	83·80	**469**	93·80
20	4·00	**70**	14·00	**120**	24·00	**170**	34·00	**220**	44·00	**270**	54·00	**320**	64·00	**370**	74·00	**420**	84·00	**470**	94·00
21	4·20	**71**	14·20	**121**	24·20	**171**	34·20	**221**	44·20	**271**	54·20	**321**	64·20	**371**	74·20	**421**	84·20	**471**	94·20
22	4·40	**72**	14·40	**122**	24·40	**172**	34·40	**222**	44·40	**272**	54·40	**322**	64·40	**372**	74·40	**422**	84·40	**472**	94·40
23	4·60	**73**	14·60	**123**	24·60	**173**	34·60	**223**	44·60	**273**	54·60	**323**	64·60	**373**	74·60	**423**	84·60	**473**	94·60
24	4·80	**74**	14·80	**124**	24·80	**174**	34·80	**224**	44·80	**274**	54·80	**324**	64·80	**374**	74·80	**424**	84·80	**474**	94·80
25	5·00	**75**	15·00	**125**	25·00	**175**	35·00	**225**	45·00	**275**	55·00	**325**	65·00	**375**	75·00	**425**	85·00	**475**	95·00
26	5·20	**76**	15·20	**126**	25·20	**176**	35·20	**226**	45·20	**276**	55·20	**326**	65·20	**376**	75·20	**426**	85·20	**476**	95·20
27	5·40	**77**	15·40	**127**	25·40	**177**	35·40	**227**	45·40	**277**	55·40	**327**	65·40	**377**	75·40	**427**	85·40	**477**	95·40
28	5·60	**78**	15·60	**128**	25·60	**178**	35·60	**228**	45·60	**278**	55·60	**328**	65·60	**378**	75·60	**428**	85·60	**478**	95·60
29	5·80	**79**	15·80	**129**	25·80	**179**	35·80	**229**	45·80	**279**	55·80	**329**	65·80	**379**	75·80	**429**	85·80	**479**	95·80
30	6·00	**80**	16·00	**130**	26·00	**180**	36·00	**230**	46·00	**280**	56·00	**330**	66·00	**380**	76·00	**430**	86·00	**480**	96·00
31	6·20	**81**	16·20	**131**	26·20	**181**	36·20	**231**	46·20	**281**	56·20	**331**	66·20	**381**	76·20	**431**	86·20	**481**	96·20
32	6·40	**82**	16·40	**132**	26·40	**182**	36·40	**232**	46·40	**282**	56·40	**332**	66·40	**382**	76·40	**432**	86·40	**482**	96·40
33	6·60	**83**	16·60	**133**	26·60	**183**	36·60	**233**	46·60	**283**	56·60	**333**	66·60	**383**	76·60	**433**	86·60	**483**	96·60
34	6·80	**84**	16·80	**134**	26·80	**184**	36·80	**234**	46·80	**284**	56·80	**334**	66·80	**384**	76·80	**434**	86·80	**484**	96·80
35	7·00	**85**	17·00	**135**	27·00	**185**	37·00	**235**	47·00	**285**	57·00	**335**	67·00	**385**	77·00	**435**	87·00	**485**	97·00
36	7·20	**86**	17·20	**136**	27·20	**186**	37·20	**236**	47·20	**286**	57·20	**336**	67·20	**386**	77·20	**436**	87·20	**486**	97·20
37	7·40	**87**	17·40	**137**	27·40	**187**	37·40	**237**	47·40	**287**	57·40	**337**	67·40	**387**	77·40	**437**	87·40	**487**	97·40
38	7·60	**88**	17·60	**138**	27·60	**188**	37·60	**238**	47·60	**288**	57·60	**338**	67·60	**388**	77·60	**438**	87·60	**488**	97·60
39	7·80	**89**	17·80	**139**	27·80	**189**	37·80	**239**	47·80	**289**	57·80	**339**	67·80	**389**	77·80	**439**	87·80	**489**	97·80
40	8·00	**90**	18·00	**140**	28·00	**190**	38·00	**240**	48·00	**290**	58·00	**340**	68·00	**390**	78·00	**440**	88·00	**490**	98·00
41	8·20	**91**	18·20	**141**	28·20	**191**	38·20	**241**	48·20	**291**	58·20	**341**	68·20	**391**	78·20	**441**	88·20	**491**	98·20
42	8·40	**92**	18·40	**142**	28·40	**192**	38·40	**242**	48·40	**292**	58·40	**342**	68·40	**392**	78·40	**442**	88·40	**492**	98·40
43	8·60	**93**	18·60	**143**	28·60	**193**	38·60	**243**	48·60	**293**	58·60	**343**	68·60	**393**	78·60	**443**	88·60	**493**	98·60
44	8·80	**94**	18·80	**144**	28·80	**194**	38·80	**244**	48·80	**294**	58·80	**344**	68·80	**394**	78·80	**444**	88·80	**494**	98·80
45	9·00	**95**	19·00	**145**	29·00	**195**	39·00	**245**	49·00	**295**	59·00	**345**	69·00	**395**	79·00	**445**	89·00	**495**	99·00
46	9·20	**96**	19·20	**146**	29·20	**196**	39·20	**246**	49·20	**296**	59·20	**346**	69·20	**396**	79·20	**446**	89·20	**496**	99·20
47	9·40	**97**	19·40	**147**	29·40	**197**	39·40	**247**	49·40	**297**	59·40	**347**	69·40	**397**	79·40	**447**	89·40	**497**	99·40
48	9·60	**98**	19·60	**148**	29·60	**198**	39·60	**248**	49·60	**298**	59·60	**348**	69·60	**398**	79·60	**448**	89·60	**498**	99·60
49	9·80	**99**	19·80	**149**	29·80	**199**	39·80	**249**	49·80	**299**	59·80	**349**	69·80	**399**	79·80	**449**	89·80	**499**	99·80
50	10·00	**100**	20·00	**150**	30·00	**200**	40·00	**250**	50·00	**300**	60·00	**350**	70·00	**400**	80·00	**450**	90·00	**500**	100·00

On Tax	**£1,000** £200	**£1,500** £300	**£2,000** £400	**£2,500** £500	**£3,000** £600	**£3,500** £700	**£4,000** £800	**£4,500** £900	**£5,000** £1,000

VAT Content of Inclusive Prices 20%

Inclusive Price £ or p	VAT @20% £ or p	Basic Price £ or p	Inclusive Price £ or p	VAT @20% £ or p	Basic Price £ or p	Inclusive Price £ or p	VAT @20% £ or p	Basic Price £ or p	Inclusive Price £ or p	VAT @20% £ or p	Basic Price £ or p	Inclusive Price £ or p	VAT @20% £ or p	Basic Price £ or p	Inclusive Price £ or p	VAT @20% £ or p	Basic Price £ or p
1	0·17	0·83	**51**	8·50	42·50	**101**	16·83	84·17	**151**	25·17	125·83	**201**	33·50	167·50	**251**	41·83	209·17
2	0·33	1·67	**52**	8·67	43·33	**102**	17·00	85·00	**152**	25·33	126·67	**202**	33·67	168·33	**252**	42·00	210·00
3	0·50	2·50	**53**	8·83	44·17	**103**	17·17	85·83	**153**	25·50	127·50	**203**	33·83	169·17	**253**	42·17	210·83
4	0·67	3·33	**54**	9·00	45·00	**104**	17·33	86·67	**154**	25·67	128·33	**204**	34·00	170·00	**254**	42·33	211·67
5	0·83	4·17	**55**	9·17	45·83	**105**	17·50	87·50	**155**	25·83	129·17	**205**	34·17	170·83	**255**	42·50	212·50
6	1·00	5·00	**56**	9·33	46·67	**106**	17·67	88·33	**156**	26·00	130·00	**206**	34·33	171·67	**256**	42·67	213·33
7	1·17	5·83	**57**	9·50	47·50	**107**	17·83	89·17	**157**	26·17	130·83	**207**	34·50	172·50	**257**	42·83	214·17
8	1·33	6·67	**58**	9·67	48·33	**108**	18·00	90·00	**158**	26·33	131·67	**208**	34·67	173·33	**258**	43·00	215·00
9	1·50	7·50	**59**	9·83	49·17	**109**	18·17	90·83	**159**	26·50	132·50	**209**	34·83	174·17	**259**	43·17	215·83
10	1·67	8·33	**60**	10·00	50·00	**110**	18·33	91·67	**160**	26·67	133·33	**210**	35·00	175·00	**260**	43·33	216·67
11	1·83	9·17	**61**	10·17	50·83	**111**	18·50	92·50	**161**	26·83	134·17	**211**	35·17	175·83	**261**	43·50	217·50
12	2·00	10·00	**62**	10·33	51·67	**112**	18·67	93·33	**162**	27·00	135·00	**212**	35·33	176·67	**262**	43·67	218·33
13	2·17	10·83	**63**	10·50	52·50	**113**	18·83	94·17	**163**	27·17	135·83	**213**	35·50	177·50	**263**	43·83	219·17
14	2·33	11·67	**64**	10·67	53·33	**114**	19·00	95·00	**164**	27·33	136·67	**214**	35·67	178·33	**264**	44·00	220·00
15	2·50	12·50	**65**	10·83	54·17	**115**	19·17	95·83	**165**	27·50	137·50	**215**	35·83	179·17	**265**	44·17	220·83
16	2·67	13·33	**66**	11·00	55·00	**116**	19·33	96·67	**166**	27·67	138·33	**216**	36·00	180·00	**266**	44·33	221·67
17	2·83	14·17	**67**	11·17	55·83	**117**	19·50	97·50	**167**	27·83	139·17	**217**	36·17	180·83	**267**	44·50	222·50
18	3·00	15·00	**68**	11·33	56·67	**118**	19·67	98·33	**168**	28·00	140·00	**218**	36·33	181·67	**268**	44·67	223·33
19	3·17	15·83	**69**	11·50	57·50	**119**	19·83	99·17	**169**	28·17	140·83	**219**	36·50	182·50	**269**	44·83	224·17
20	3·33	16·67	**70**	11·67	58·33	**120**	20·00	100·00	**170**	28·33	141·67	**220**	36·67	183·33	**270**	45·00	225·00
21	3·50	17·50	**71**	11·83	59·17	**121**	20·17	100·83	**171**	28·50	142·50	**221**	36·83	184·17	**271**	45·17	225·83
22	3·67	18·33	**72**	12·00	60·00	**122**	20·33	101·67	**172**	28·67	143·33	**222**	37·00	185·00	**272**	45·33	226·67
23	3·83	19·17	**73**	12·17	60·83	**123**	20·50	102·50	**173**	28·83	144·17	**223**	37·17	185·83	**273**	45·50	227·50
24	4·00	20·00	**74**	12·33	61·67	**124**	20·67	103·33	**174**	29·00	145·00	**224**	37·33	186·67	**274**	45·67	228·33
25	4·17	20·83	**75**	12·50	62·50	**125**	20·83	104·17	**175**	29·17	145·83	**225**	37·50	187·50	**275**	45·83	229·17
26	4·33	21·67	**76**	12·67	63·33	**126**	21·00	105·00	**176**	29·33	146·67	**226**	37·67	188·33	**276**	46·00	230·00
27	4·50	22·50	**77**	12·83	64·17	**127**	21·17	105·83	**177**	29·50	147·50	**227**	37·83	189·17	**277**	46·17	230·83
28	4·67	23·33	**78**	13·00	65·00	**128**	21·33	106·67	**178**	29·67	148·33	**228**	38·00	190·00	**278**	46·33	231·67
29	4·83	24·17	**79**	13·17	65·83	**129**	21·50	107·50	**179**	29·83	149·17	**229**	38·17	190·83	**279**	46·50	232·50
30	5·00	25·00	**80**	13·33	66·67	**130**	21·67	108·33	**180**	30·00	150·00	**230**	38·33	191·67	**280**	46·67	233·33
31	5·17	25·83	**81**	13·50	67·50	**131**	21·83	109·17	**181**	30·17	150·83	**231**	38·50	192·50	**281**	46·83	234·17
32	5·33	26·67	**82**	13·67	68·33	**132**	22·00	110·00	**182**	30·33	151·67	**232**	38·67	193·33	**282**	47·00	235·00
33	5·50	27·50	**83**	13·83	69·17	**133**	22·17	110·83	**183**	30·50	152·50	**233**	38·83	194·17	**283**	47·17	235·83
34	5·67	28·33	**84**	14·00	70·00	**134**	22·33	111·67	**184**	30·67	153·33	**234**	39·00	195·00	**284**	47·33	236·67
35	5·83	29·17	**85**	14·17	70·83	**135**	22·50	112·50	**185**	30·83	154·17	**235**	39·17	195·83	**285**	47·50	237·50
36	6·00	30·00	**86**	14·33	71·67	**136**	22·67	113·33	**186**	31·00	155·00	**236**	39·33	196·67	**286**	47·67	238·33
37	6·17	30·83	**87**	14·50	72·50	**137**	22·83	114·17	**187**	31·17	155·83	**237**	39·50	197·50	**287**	47·83	239·17
38	6·33	31·67	**88**	14·67	73·33	**138**	23·00	115·00	**188**	31·33	156·67	**238**	39·67	198·33	**288**	48·00	240·00
39	6·50	32·50	**89**	14·83	74·17	**139**	23·17	115·83	**189**	31·50	157·50	**239**	39·83	199·17	**289**	48·17	240·83
40	6·67	33·33	**90**	15·00	75·00	**140**	23·33	116·67	**190**	31·67	158·33	**240**	40·00	200·00	**290**	48·33	241·67
41	6·83	34·17	**91**	15·17	75·83	**141**	23·50	117·50	**191**	31·83	159·17	**241**	40·17	200·83	**291**	48·50	242·50
42	7·00	35·00	**92**	15·33	76·67	**142**	23·67	118·33	**192**	32·00	160·00	**242**	40·33	201·67	**292**	48·67	243·33
43	7·17	35·83	**93**	15·50	77·50	**143**	23·83	119·17	**193**	32·17	160·83	**243**	40·50	202·50	**293**	48·83	244·17
44	7·33	36·67	**94**	15·67	78·33	**144**	24·00	120·00	**194**	32·33	161·67	**244**	40·67	203·33	**294**	49·00	245·00
45	7·50	37·50	**95**	15·83	79·17	**145**	24·17	120·83	**195**	32·50	162·50	**245**	40·83	204·17	**295**	49·17	245·83
46	7·67	38·33	**96**	16·00	80·00	**146**	24·33	121·67	**196**	32·67	163·33	**246**	41·00	205·00	**296**	49·33	246·67
47	7·83	39·17	**97**	16·17	80·83	**147**	24·50	122·50	**197**	32·83	164·17	**247**	41·17	205·83	**297**	49·50	247·50
48	8·00	40·00	**98**	16·33	81·67	**148**	24·67	123·33	**198**	33·00	165·00	**248**	41·33	206·67	**298**	49·67	248·33
49	8·17	40·83	**99**	16·50	82·50	**149**	24·83	124·17	**199**	33·17	165·83	**249**	41·50	207·50	**299**	49·83	249·17
50	8·33	41·67	**100**	16·67	83·33	**150**	25·00	125·00	**200**	33·33	166·67	**250**	41·67	208·33	**300**	50·00	250·00
500	83·33	416·67	**600**	100·00	500·00	**700**	116·67	583·33	**800**	133·33	666·67	**900**	150·00	750·00	**1,000**	166·67	833·33

Number of days Table: Tax Year

Years other than leap years

(Quarter days are highlighted)

	April		May		June		July		August		September		October		November		December		January		February		March		
Days	lapsed	to go	lapsed	to go	lapsed	to go	lapsed	to go	lapsed	to go	lapsed	to go	lapsed	to go	lapsed	to go	lapsed	to go	lapsed	to go	lapsed	to go	lapsed	to go	Days
1	361	4	26	339	57	308	87	278	118	247	149	216	179	186	210	155	240	125	271	94	302	63	330	35	**1**
2	362	3	27	338	58	307	88	277	119	246	150	215	180	185	211	154	241	124	272	93	303	62	331	34	**2**
3	363	2	28	337	59	306	89	276	120	245	151	214	181	184	212	153	242	123	273	92	304	61	332	33	**3**
4	364	1	29	336	60	305	90	275	121	244	152	213	182	183	213	152	243	122	274	91	305	60	333	32	**4**
5	365	0	30	335	61	304	91	274	122	243	153	212	183	182	214	151	244	121	275	90	306	59	334	31	**5**
6	1	364	31	334	62	303	92	273	123	242	154	211	184	181	215	150	245	120	276	89	307	58	335	30	**6**
7	2	363	32	333	63	302	93	272	124	241	155	210	185	180	216	149	246	119	277	88	308	57	336	29	**7**
8	3	362	33	332	64	301	94	271	125	240	156	209	186	179	217	148	247	118	278	87	309	56	337	28	**8**
9	4	361	34	331	65	300	95	270	126	239	157	208	187	178	218	147	248	117	279	86	310	55	338	27	**9**
10	5	360	35	330	66	299	96	269	127	238	158	207	188	177	219	146	249	116	280	85	311	54	339	26	**10**
11	6	359	36	329	67	298	97	268	128	237	159	206	189	176	220	145	250	115	281	84	312	53	340	25	**11**
12	7	358	37	328	68	297	98	267	129	236	160	205	190	175	221	144	251	114	282	83	313	52	341	24	**12**
13	8	357	38	327	69	296	99	266	130	235	161	204	191	174	222	143	252	113	283	82	314	51	342	23	**13**
14	9	356	39	326	70	295	100	265	131	234	162	203	192	173	223	142	253	112	284	81	315	50	343	22	**14**
15	10	355	40	325	71	294	101	264	132	233	163	202	193	172	224	141	254	111	285	80	316	49	344	21	**15**
16	11	354	41	324	72	293	102	263	133	232	164	201	194	171	225	140	255	110	286	79	317	48	345	20	**16**
17	12	353	42	323	73	292	103	262	134	231	165	200	195	170	226	139	256	109	287	78	318	47	346	19	**17**
18	13	352	43	322	74	291	104	261	135	230	166	199	196	169	227	138	257	108	288	77	319	46	347	18	**18**
19	14	351	44	321	75	290	105	260	136	229	167	198	197	168	228	137	258	107	289	76	320	45	348	17	**19**
20	15	350	45	320	76	289	106	259	137	228	168	197	198	167	229	136	259	106	290	75	321	44	349	16	**20**
21	16	349	46	319	77	288	107	258	138	227	169	196	199	166	230	135	260	105	291	74	322	43	350	15	**21**
22	17	348	47	318	78	287	108	257	139	226	170	195	200	165	231	134	261	104	292	73	323	42	351	14	**22**
23	18	347	48	317	79	286	109	256	140	225	171	194	201	164	232	133	262	103	293	72	324	41	352	13	**23**
24	19	346	49	316	**80**	**285**	110	255	141	224	172	193	202	163	233	132	263	102	294	71	325	40	353	12	**24**
25	20	345	50	315	81	284	111	254	142	223	173	192	203	162	234	131	**264**	**101**	295	70	326	39	**354**	**11**	**25**
26	21	344	51	314	82	283	112	253	143	222	174	191	204	161	235	130	265	100	296	69	327	38	355	10	**26**
27	22	343	52	313	83	282	113	252	144	221	175	190	205	160	236	129	266	99	297	68	328	37	356	9	**27**
28	23	342	53	312	84	281	114	251	145	220	176	189	206	159	237	128	267	98	298	67	329	36	357	8	**28**
29	24	341	54	311	85	280	115	250	146	219	**177**	**188**	207	158	238	127	268	97	299	66			358	7	**29**
30	25	340	55	310	86	279	116	249	147	218	178	187	208	157	239	126	269	96	300	65			359	6	**30**
31			56	309			117	248	148	217			209	156			270	95	301	64			360	5	**31**

Number of days Table: Tax Year

Leap years falling within tax years 2019/2020 2023/24 2027/28

(Quarter days are highlighted)

	April		May		June		July		August		September		October		November		December		January		February		March		
Days	lapsed	to go	lapsed	to go	lapsed	to go	lapsed	to go	lapsed	to go	lapsed	to go	lapsed	to go	lapsed	to go	lapsed	to go	lapsed	to go	lapsed	to go	lapsed	to go	**Days**
1	362	4	26	340	57	309	87	279	118	248	149	217	179	187	210	156	240	126	271	95	302	64	331	35	**1**
2	363	3	27	339	58	308	88	278	119	247	150	216	180	186	211	155	241	125	272	94	303	63	332	34	**2**
3	364	2	28	338	59	307	89	277	120	246	151	215	181	185	212	154	242	124	273	93	304	62	333	33	**3**
4	365	1	29	337	60	306	90	276	121	245	152	214	182	184	213	153	243	123	274	92	305	61	334	32	**4**
5	366	0	30	336	61	305	91	275	122	244	153	213	183	183	214	152	244	122	275	91	306	60	335	31	**5**
6	1	365	31	335	62	304	92	274	123	243	154	212	184	182	215	151	245	121	276	90	307	59	336	30	**6**
7	2	364	32	334	63	303	93	273	124	242	155	211	185	181	216	150	246	120	277	89	308	58	337	29	**7**
8	3	363	33	333	64	302	94	272	125	241	156	210	186	180	217	149	247	119	278	88	309	57	338	28	**8**
9	4	362	34	332	65	301	95	271	126	240	157	209	187	179	218	148	248	118	279	87	310	56	339	27	**9**
10	5	361	35	331	66	300	96	270	127	239	158	208	188	178	219	147	249	117	280	86	311	55	340	26	**10**
11	6	360	36	330	67	299	97	269	128	238	159	207	189	177	220	146	250	116	281	85	312	54	341	25	**11**
12	7	359	37	329	68	298	98	268	129	237	160	206	190	176	221	145	251	115	282	84	313	53	342	24	**12**
13	8	358	38	328	69	297	99	267	130	236	161	205	191	175	222	144	252	114	283	83	314	52	343	23	**13**
14	9	357	39	327	70	296	100	266	131	235	162	204	192	174	223	143	253	113	284	82	315	51	344	22	**14**
15	10	356	40	326	71	295	101	265	132	234	163	203	193	173	224	142	254	112	285	81	316	50	345	21	**15**
16	11	355	41	325	72	294	102	264	133	233	164	202	194	172	225	141	255	111	286	80	317	49	346	20	**16**
17	12	354	42	324	73	293	103	263	134	232	165	201	195	171	226	140	256	110	287	79	318	48	347	19	**17**
18	13	353	43	323	74	292	104	262	135	231	166	200	196	170	227	139	257	109	288	78	319	47	348	18	**18**
19	14	352	44	322	75	291	105	261	136	230	167	199	197	169	228	138	258	108	289	77	320	46	349	17	**19**
20	15	351	45	321	76	290	106	260	137	229	168	198	198	168	229	137	259	107	290	76	321	45	350	16	**20**
21	16	350	46	320	77	289	107	259	138	228	169	197	199	167	230	136	260	106	291	75	322	44	351	15	**21**
22	17	349	47	319	78	288	108	258	139	227	170	196	200	166	231	135	261	105	292	74	323	43	352	14	**22**
23	18	348	48	318	79	287	109	257	140	226	171	195	201	165	232	134	262	104	293	73	324	42	353	13	**23**
24	19	347	49	317	**80**	**286**	110	256	141	225	172	194	202	164	233	133	263	103	294	72	325	41	354	12	**24**
25	20	346	50	316	81	285	111	255	142	224	173	193	203	163	234	132	**264**	**102**	295	71	326	40	**355**	**11**	**25**
26	21	345	51	315	82	284	112	254	143	223	174	192	204	162	235	131	265	101	296	70	327	39	356	10	**26**
27	22	344	52	314	83	283	113	253	144	222	175	191	205	161	236	130	266	100	297	69	328	38	357	9	**27**
28	23	343	53	313	84	282	114	252	145	221	176	190	206	150	237	129	267	99	298	68	329	37	358	8	**28**
29	24	342	54	312	85	281	115	251	146	220	**177**	**189**	207	159	238	128	268	98	299	67	330	36	359	7	**29**
30	25	341	55	311	86	280	116	250	147	219	178	188	208	158	239	127	269	97	300	66			360	6	**30**
31			56	310			117	249	148	218			209	157			270	96	301	65			361	5	**31**

Tax Year Planner 2019/20

	April	May	June	July	August	Sept	Oct	Nov	Dec	Jan	Feb	March	April	
Mon	1			1										Mon
Tue	2			2			1							Tue
Wed	3	1		3			2			1			1	Wed
Thurs	4	2		4	1		3			2			2	Thurs
Fri	5	3		5	2		4	1		3			3	Fri
Sat	6	4	1	6	3		5	2		4	1		4	Sat
Sun	7	5	2	7	4	1	6	3	1	5	2	1	5	Sun
Mon	8	6	3	8	5	2	7	4	2	6	3	2	6	Mon
Tue	9	7	4	9	6	3	8	5	3	7	4	3	7	Tue
Wed	10	8	5	10	7	4	9	6	4	8	5	4	8	Wed
Thurs	11	9	6	11	8	5	10	7	5	9	6	5	9	Thurs
Fri	12	10	7	12	9	6	11	8	6	10	7	6	10	Fri
Sat	13	11	8	13	10	7	12	9	7	11	8	7	11	Sat
Sun	14	12	9	14	11	8	13	10	8	12	9	8	12	Sun
Mon	15	13	10	15	12	9	14	11	9	13	10	9	13	Mon
Tue	16	14	11	16	13	10	15	12	10	14	11	10	14	Tue
Wed	17	15	12	17	14	11	16	13	11	15	12	11	15	Wed
Thurs	18	16	13	18	15	12	17	14	12	16	13	12	16	Thurs
Fri	19	17	14	19	16	13	18	15	13	17	14	13	17	Fri
Sat	20	18	15	20	17	14	19	16	14	18	15	14	18	Sat
Sun	21	19	16	21	18	15	20	17	15	19	16	15	19	Sun
Mon	22	20	17	22	19	16	21	18	16	20	17	16	20	Mon
Tue	23	21	18	23	20	17	22	19	17	21	18	17	21	Tue
Wed	24	22	19	24	21	18	23	20	18	22	19	18	22	Wed
Thurs	25	23	20	25	22	19	24	21	19	23	20	19	23	Thurs
Fri	26	24	21	26	23	20	25	22	20	24	21	20	24	Fri
Sat	27	25	22	27	24	21	26	23	21	25	22	21	25	Sat
Sun	28	26	23	28	25	22	27	24	22	26	23	22	26	Sun
Mon	29	27	24	29	26	23	28	25	23	27	24	23	27	Mon
Tue	30	28	25	30	27	24	29	26	24	28	25	24	28	Tue
Wed		29	26	31	28	25	30	27	25	29	26	25	29	Wed
Thurs		30	27		29	26	31	28	26	30	27	26	30	Thurs
Fri		31	28		30	27		29	27	31	28	27		Fri
Sat			29		31	28		30	28		29	28		Sat
Sun			30			29			29			29		Sun
Mon						30			30			30		Mon
Tue									31			31		Tue

Notes

Notes